IMPERFECT PARTNERS

Dean Hitchman

ISBN 978-1-0980-8556-8 (paperback)
ISBN 978-1-0980-8557-5 (digital)

Christian Faith Publishing, Inc.
832 Park Avenue
Meadville, PA 16335
www.christianfaithpublishing.com

Printed in the United States of America

It is reported that Americans are addicted to sports. In 1992, the average American household watched 178 hours of sports on television, over three hours per week. Sports pages in American newspapers "far outnumber" those devoted to movies, theater, sciences, and art combined. Advertisers spend more than $3.7 billion a year sponsoring sporting events, and our education system makes a huge investment in physical education so that nearly every child in the country can participate in sport at school.

It is reported that many Americans "know more about sport than we do about politics, science, technology, economics, or their own Constitution. We discuss sport with friends, relatives, and strangers more quickly and intensely, with more passion and conviction, than any other subject." And, may I add, knowledge. In many cases, fans can recite who won or lost for all preceding years over the last decade or longer.

Most studies report that leisure time has remained relatively constant since 1975. A statistic such as this would not give cause for us to pay attention but rather passing it off as just another trend associated with the times in which we live, or is there an underlying reason for leisure time to have topped out?

Those of us who are old enough to remember, and if we older folks are still able to remember the television series that ran around 1949–1958 "The Life of Riley," we can see it was the classic depiction of the average American family. "The Life of Riley" depicted Chester Riley—played by William Bendix—as the sole breadwinner of a family of four who would come home to his family and homemaker spouse after a day of hard work at the aircraft plant as a Riveter.

Upon bursting through the front door, he would proclaim in a loud voice, "PEG, I'M HOME!" Riley's fast-paced energetic entrance was always the kickoff that set the tone for the rest of the show, usually leading to Riley getting in hot water. By the end of the show, amends were made and viewers were left with a sense of "It's a wonderful life" and with a sense of fulfillment and looking forward to the following week's episode.

Statistics indicate that today Americans are working harder and longer, often holding two and three part-time jobs just to keep up with the same standard of living as the one-breadwinner job in the heyday of the industrial revolution era and "The Life of Riley."

The traditional one-income family slowly but surely began noticeably receding in the late 1960s and was well under way by the early 1970s. It resembled the coming in and going out of the ocean tide, something you almost don't even notice. Except the American economy was the tide with a one-way ticket to other places to be determined by corporate America and nonetheless the help of our very own United States congressmen and congresswomen from both political parties and under multiple administrations.

The one-income family was more the norm then and "The Life of Riley" explains that time in history very well about the average American family. By following unfolding economic events that would begin to transpire and transform our whole American culture, "The Life of Riley" gives us a clear panoramic view of what economic and social life in America was like following World War II forward, until around the conclusion of the Vietnam War. Economic America was about to take a downward drift that would change the landscape of America forever.

It is never talked about in any terms that points the finger of blame on every administration—Republican or Democratic—for cutting deals that allowed corporate America such freedom of trade that would gut the American economy and leave American workers on the sidelines. If you ever wondered how a politician could go into office "penniless," relatively speaking, and leave a multimillionaire, the spear-carrying lobbyists for the corporations are very likely a part of the reason.

By the late 1960s onward, as odd as it may seem, rock-and-roll music, free love, and illicit drugs to turn on, tune in, and drop out were dramatically altering the makeup of American society.

Divorce was increasing, day care was springing up, jobs and pay were taking a nosedive, workers were (immigrating internally) following jobs, and the two-income family was emerging as the new norm. Americans were indeed working harder, often holding down more than one job and earning less.

The erosion of our economic system based largely on our manufacturing gigantism was slowly being handed over to what could be described as second-class nations with cheaper labor forces, lax environmental laws, and backward nations ruled by despotic leaders who were a threat even to their own people, selling them out almost as slave labor to the capitalists.

Hindsight seems to indicate that the American middle class had lost their sense of purpose and had given up hope toward self-sufficiency, thereby adjusting to circumstances by drifting aimlessly toward a life of debauchery. A new era was settling in on America, as American corporations pulled the plug in their bid for the lowest-cost labor forces available on the planet. It must be stated as a reminder, the fundamental responsibility of Congress is to protect the American people. If anything could be lacking in this respect, it was that this responsibility was not only lacking but also totally absent from any governmental agenda.

If I am successful in projecting only one thing in this entire book to my readers, it is this: What is the responsibility of our sitting Congresses? The responsibility of those being voted into office by we, the people, is to be advocates, custodians, and protectors, literally and figuratively, of the American people. There is no responsibility of our elected officials that carries greater importance than this, as you will come to appreciate as we bring forward the reasoning for titling this book *Imperfect Partners*.

A Quickening Pace in the 1970s Yesteryear

When the trend of outsourcing began catching on, it amounted to subcontracting (in-house) activities, mostly to independent or non-union vendors. The affected industries wasted little time in expanding to a larger role of (exporting) production capacity.

The effects were immediate for many workers being (uprooted) from what used to be secure employment with a good company for a lifetime. The life of Riley was changing, and changing rapidly!

Free market globalization has a ring about it that just by saying it makes you feel somehow that the emerging new global economy is akin to a speeding train that cannot be stopped. Just by interjecting the word *global* in conversation denotes limitations on any one-world entity voicing opposition to the principle of participation.

If any one nation had the audacity to hold out, opposing the ideal of globalization, safeguards were put in place to limit the naysayers. What were the safeguards? Specifically the World Trade Organization (WTO), the United Nations (UN), and the International Monetary Fund (IMF) are three of the power brokers enacted to persuade all nations to observe the rules of engagement to do business in the new global economy.

We will be reviewing the WTO, UN, and IMF in more detail as to their role in the global economy. The enigma surrounding these world organizations is that their functional appearances is that they were created to promote harmony and benevolent interaction among global trading partners. What were these organizations able to achieve? For one thing, and maybe the primary thing that they did do, especially the WTO, was that it made the US Congress look innocent of responsibility for international trade and powerless to protect the American economy. In other words, it made Congress look like "It's out of our hands," don't fault us for the hand dealt us!

Free trade was clearly a one-way street that posed the most expensive arrangement imaginable for the health and well-being of the American economy and the working middle class in particular. Was Washington asleep at the wheel?

It goes to show that our government did a good job of selling middle America on the concept that free enterprise was something outside of their control. It was an accepted ideal that free trade was just something to be tolerated whether you liked it or not. The fact is that *all* commerce between nations is very much a leadership role—that is, unless those in control choose to do nothing to manage that which is in their job description and is within their jurisdiction.

The truth of the matter is that when the wholesale export of America's manufacturing base was being exported, every sitting American Congress, one after another, participated in crafting trade deals and writing policy at the urging of investors while our elected officials nodded in approval for lobbyists not to worry, "We will take care of you." And so the selling of America commenced and remained uninterrupted for *four decades*.

America as a Child Learning to Walk

In earlier times, when America was in its infancy, there was nothing wrong with the government working hand in hand with those who had money to spend toward the development of any and every business and building infrastructure. America had so little of everything in finished goods that many things were handmade, one of its kind, one at a time. In that time frame, you could honestly say that trickle-down economics did work and was welcomed.

The American worker welcomed anyone who had enough wealth to invest in creating businesses that would provide jobs and economic opportunity, opening the doors to prosperity for all. Indeed, America was an emerging economy, by definition.

America was growing, inventing, increasing, and becoming producers and consumers. The time was right, and it was the right thing to do (for the time being). America was sitting on top of an abundance of water, timber, iron ore, coal—all the raw materials and resources needed to produce infrastructure and supply industries on a twenty-four-hour seven-day-week work schedule.

Modern-Day Ground Travel, Faster than Yesterday's Air Travel

At a time in history when technology was gaining speed on par with the modern-day French bullet train, simply labeled TGV (Train Grande Vitesse), with a recorded speed of 357.2 mph in April 2007. The point is that technology has been gaining speed—a lot of speed.

The world was moving in many directions, and corporate America was taking advantage of the opportunity of a lifetime. Moving production offshore. *The time had come for our Congress to change their relationship with the corporations from that of enabler to that of overseer.* Obviously, we the people know the course of action they chose. You won't hear it from anywhere else that I know of that our very own Congress enabled the gutting of American manufacturing to leave American workers sitting on the sidelines, but that is exactly what happened, and they alone are responsible for the incompetent and negligent actions that I describe as economic terrorism driven by political pandering on America.

When responsibility to thwart off the onslaught of economic annihilation such as passing off global trade as a way to explain away congressional action of do nothing to protect American economic interest and jobs, is nothing short of a form of terrorism when you take into consideration that millions of American workers were forced to uproot and relocate every part of their lives, and usually at a lower standard; Such a drastic resettlement requirement is nothing short of perpetrated terrorism on a people in favor of cowing down to special interest. It was very low-key. Nonetheless, we must look at the results that the action produced. Economic annihilation of an entire class of people: if that doesn't amount to a form of terrorism, what does?

Managing Is as Critical as the Invention

As with anything, speed needs the technology to ensure safety by developing a system or systems that appropriately manage or harness the systems. In the case of managing such a powerful invention as the French bullet train, the creators must have considered every detail as being of critical importance, from the most simplistic things as wheel-bearing type, quality, lubricant, the track system, and guidance systems to ensure that the track is clear for a required stopping distance, etc., etc.

When America got economically "rolling," Washington should have gotten rolling too. Their role and partnership with corporate America should have gradually and steadily changed to meet the need of adolescent America moving into adulthood. However, as adept as our founding fathers were in laying the groundwork for protections and freedoms of "We the people" for theirs and future generations, it seems that American politics became more and more insensitive about their role and more sensitive to personal opportunities.

A child's needs are far different from those of an adult. As corporate America grew amassing prominence and power, politics continued to deal with them as a (spoiled) child, giving them what they want versus now providing them with what they need. In a free-market system, obviously there was a need for a relationship paradigm shift from nurturing to managing. Almost everyone is familiar with the term "Too big to fail." It sounds like our little boy has gotten too big to control.

The Competent and Committed
Know the Importance

There are many extreme differences between nurturing and managing that are important to you as a reader to think about and consider in understanding the right kind of political intervention for a nation that is emerging and a nation that has emerged or matured.

Competent management is also the determining factor as to whether we are maintaining proper balance within our systems that serve our economic and social needs simultaneously and appropriately.

Let us be reminded again: It is the responsibility of our Congresses to manage international trade, and it is also the responsibility of our Congresses to protect the American people. That has an all-inclusive meaning to include trade as well as protection from foreign enemies. One of these responsibilities carries no more weight than the other, and when the two merge, as in the case of the global economy, capitalism has the right to flourish but not at the expense of annihilating American workers.

We will be investigating the evolution of industrialization leading up to globalization and the results it has produced along the way. On the journey, we will frequently check the report card and grade our leadership accordingly for fairness, equality, and economic justice for all.

The United States has a trade deficit with *every one* of her trade partners. Later, we will take a look at the actual deficit statistics. Why does our leadership even endorse such poor trade policies and allow such out-of-balance trade deficits that is depleting our national treasure? Even worse, these government-endorsed policies are guaranteed to swiftly and assuredly lead to a major loss of jobs and shrinking middle-class America.

There is only one explainable reason why our lawmakers have bent over to accommodate corporate America: it is to ensure that corporate investment in the global arena can obtain insurmountable profits at the same time line Congressional ignoramus's pockets. This could not and would not have happened if our sitting Congresses had been doing their job of *managing* our international trade through fair trade rather than free trade, thereby protecting the American worker. Consequently, they sold out America economically, again ensuring that the wealthy get richer and the poor continue to add to their numbers.

I will offer my readers documented information from professionals and data to substantiate the many allegations we will discuss. It matters very little what we as individuals may believe, unless it is backed up by evidence to support those beliefs and substance as to what the record really shows.

Don't let your focus become confused with all the issues we will discuss as we proceed by wondering what this has to do with the decline of the middle class in America, or why this author boldly uses the term *economic* and *political terrorism* interchangeably. Believe me, most of the topics discussed in this book has everything to do with why America is declining in the world arena.

Is there really ten cents' worth of difference between Republicans and Democrats?

For instance, after Democratic president Bill Clinton granted China most-favored-nation status, MFN, he proceeded to boast about new trade that supported 150,000 American jobs as a result of his brave act. What he didn't tell, however, was that America lost over 2 million jobs during the exact time, all of which went to China.

It must be noted that, initially, Clinton resisted granting this status, citing China's record on human rights abuses, weapons proliferation, etc. However, eventually he capitulated. I wonder why. You don't suppose it had more to do with American investment by American corporations importing their own goods produced with Chinese labor back to America at huge profits.

Even though Mr. Clinton is a Democrat, one has to wonder what made him soften his principles concerning China's belligerence toward their own people. It couldn't possibly be corporate-influence money or a bogus speaking opportunity, could it?

For most twentieth century workers, working for the same employer for thirty to forty years is almost unheard of. This relatively new culture and shifting economy, at its inception, was made tolerable in large part because the jobs being terminated were a trickle in comparison to the might of America's productive capacity.

Initially, outsourcing garnered rank and file acceptance by reason that many union workers bought into the premise that it was a way to strengthen their sector position, hold on to a greater number of their jobs, and as long as the core business remained intact, it enhanced job security.

In fact, the concept of maintaining the health of the core business was the emphasis that won over employee support and willingness for belt tightening on pay raises, agreeing to benefits concessions, etc., at contract time. It was always a case of dealing with the inevitable, which was shoring up the core business.

The only thing was, the core business eventually disappeared too. Do you think maybe we, the American workers, were being lied to in the form of song and dance to sell their agenda? The agenda was to make sure that everyone was convinced that we were a part of this new emerging global economy and nothing or no one could alter that!

The curtain was swiftly closing on the life of Riley.

Shortly after, 1970 corporate America deploys the scalpel

If you ever witnessed a young boy with a new shiny, sharp pocket knife, you would see he would pick up a fresh tree sapling a couple of feet long and start whittling. You know the result. In fairly short order, the stick becomes so short that there is nothing left of the stick to hold on to, let alone whittle down.

That is exactly the way every sitting Congress managed international trade. They stood by and nodded to lobbyists, filled their campaign coffers, and sold their constituency on the idea that it is the result of the new global economy, as if their hands were tied to do anything to alter such a disastrous outcome.

The unions were at a disadvantage because of jurisdictional limitations and were further hampered by political standing by the side of big business and declining to do anything to manage free trade.

Looking back on this situation, I have asked myself repeatedly if we the people even realized that Congress was responsible for protecting American interests in the global economy. Any American workers who may have expected government intervention amounted to the Bay of Pigs.

How was the US government's handling of international commerce similar to the Bay of Pigs invasion? Read on. The two are so similar it is mind-boggling.

Bay of Pigs Invasion: 1961

Source: http://www.britannica.com/blogs/2009/01/4-kennedys-failure-at-the-bay-of-pigs-top-10-mistakes-by-us-presidents/

Ideally, the president (Kennedy) would have liked the invasion and the overthrow of Castro to appear to be the work entirely of the Cuban exile community. He wanted to be able to deny that the US government had had a hand in any of it.

But Dulles and Bissell realized the "noise" was essential to this mission: if US aircraft would not support the Cuban brigade from the air, and if there were no US battleships off-shore full of US troops ready to back up the exile fighters, then the invasion was likely to fail. The presence of the US military was the key to a successful invasion and a successful uprising of Cubans disenchanted with the Castro regime.

But neither Dulles nor Bissell revealed their worries to the president. And there was one more point they failed to mention and which Kennedy may or may not have known: with 200,000 troops and militia at his disposal, Castro would have no trouble disposing of 1,300 volunteers, most of whom had no battlefield experience.

Many of the approximately 1,300 CIA-trained Cuban exiles believed fervently that they were the first wave of Cuban freedom fighters who would liberate their homeland from

Castro. They were convinced that as they stormed ashore they would be supported overhead by some of the finest fighter pilots of the US Air Force, and as they advanced into Cuba, the US Marines would be right behind them. These men were sorely mistaken.

On April 14, 1961, just three days before the invasion, Kennedy called Bissell to ask how many planes he would use in the operation. Bissell told the president the CIA planned to use all sixteen of their B-26s.

"Well, I don't want it on that scale," Kennedy replied. "I want it minimal."

So Bissell cut the number of planes for the invasion to eight. The next day, those eight planes attacked the three airfields of the Cuban air force, knocking out some of the aircraft but not enough to cripple the enemy. Already the invasion was off to a bad start.

Early in the morning of April 17, 1961, the 1,300 Cuban exiles waded ashore at the Bay of Pigs and were very quickly pinned down by Cuban fighter planes. The eight American B-26s gave the men on the beach forty minutes of air cover, then pulled out. With the sea at their backs, no means of retreat, and no chance of advancing into the interior of Cuba, the brigade was in a desperate position.

Back in Washington, the CIA and the Kennedy administration concluded that the invasion would fail. In a conversation with his brother Robert Kennedy, the president said he wished he had permitted the use of US ships to back up the Cuban exiles.

"I'd rather be an aggressor," he said, "than a bum."

Why was the Bay of Pigs similar to the plight of American jobs being exported? It has the identical earmarks *for lack of any meaningful support from those who could make a difference.*

Coinciding with What Was Happening— Washington Should Have Reacted Through Up-to-Date Management of the Emerging Global Economy

Right from the start, when corporate America found it lucrative to export American jobs and treasure, Washington should have had the foresight to react to what was an easily distinguishable situation and implement trade policies that were in the *best interest of American workers in particular and America's national security concurrently.*

Again, if Washington bureaucrats were interested in protecting America's position as a superpower among nations, initiate global leadership, support our middle class, and at the same time bringing prosperity to backward nations), they had the perfect opportunity to implement those ideals. Instead, they chose to do nothing that would hinder the multinational investors' agenda. In their failure to act, they miserably failed America's interest at the behest of corporate communism. It indeed amounted to our domestic economic Bay of Pigs.

At about 1970 Onward It Was Downhill All the Way

The whittling effect of American jobs and America's wealth would continue unabated until the terminal realization set in: there was little left. "Made in China" was now the norm.

"Strengthening the core business" was an operating phrase that I believe most middle managers were sincere about and truly supported outsourcing to generate higher numbers in black ink. The viewpoint in many instances was we are eliminating parts of the business that are incompatible with the core business, are unprofitable, or we no longer believe those are good businesses for the organization.

I believe that in the early stages of outsourcing many employees in the private sector sincerely believed they were doing the right thing to cut waste, strengthen profitability, and make their companies more secure in the long term. Indeed, it did improve the position of the companies, but it only prolonged the agony for fewer workers left who were working harder for less, until the company pulled the plug altogether in many cases. "Made in America" became the exception rather than the rule.

In many respects, it resembled what George W. Bush's views were to excuse his inaction or inability to address immigration from our southern border. Bush often stated, "They are only doing jobs that American workers are unwilling to do."

For those who bought in to this policy, as a core value or only what shows on the surface, many may well be nodding their heads in agreement, convinced that they have nothing to lose.

Have you ever watched HGTV (Home Makeover) on Saturday mornings and observed what ethnic groups of people are doing the work on the construction sites? Immigrant Hispanics are in the majority, are they not? Either George W. Bush is wrong, or I am in error for believing that Americans are unwilling to do construction work.

Green-card holders replacing US-born or naturalized citizens is a much-broader issue than just looking at crop pickers and construction work being done by immigrants.

Our American corporate friends are out front and a long way ahead of what most Americans are familiar with in terms of first choice with foreign nationals from many other places at cheaper labor rates. This huge issue can and is often referred to by politicians themselves as a broken government!

Broken government is what is (hidden) in the problems of immigration. Migrant workers, as we the American middle-class know it, can honestly say that migrant workers are making a huge impact on driving down wages in most any economic sector. The rich and powerful like our immigration policy just the way it is, and that is why nothing is being done to change the "Take no action policy" that will interfere with devaluing work.

Let's remember, all work is of value no matter what it is. Work has value and must be done by someone. What corporate America has been successful of doing is convincing we the people that some work is of such low value that the Department of Labor even makes allowances for employers to pay less-than-minimum wages.

Furthermore they have ingrained the premise that some work is outside the norm as unacceptable in American culture. Therefore, we should expect whatever work they label as subpar is good enough for someone from somewhere else. *This viewpoint has all the earmarks of elitism, cultural bigotry, and racial demagoguery.* But the American populace by and large have ignored this viewpoint, or simply nodded their heads in tacit agreement with what leadership has been projecting to substantiate and support leadership politics' failure to upset their corporate friends by going forward with a policy that actually values people relative to corporate profits.

Re-ac-tion-ary: "extreme conservatism or rightism in politics, opposing political or social change." While the dictionary describes *reactionary* as a conservative characteristic, it is applicable to both modern-day political parties by reason that they have had a hundred years of practicing ideological entrenchment. When all is said and done or, as the standard saying goes, "at the end of the day," neither is working the most fervent for those who pony up hefty bonus money: corporate America!

Reactionary best describes how our government works under either political parties. In spite of what they may say they work very diligently to prove they are right, they oppose most any change that may, can, or will be for the good of "We the people," and they most certainly are opposed to changing anything that may affect or alter their own personal gain.

As we continue on throughout this book, you will be looking at many aspects of why ultra-capitalism or corporate communism (author's words) is doing so well and democracy (lite) is doing so poorly toward economic equality in industrialized nations and moving developing societies from poverty to prosperity *at the slowest rate possible*.

Considering the tremendous investment that American corporations have placed in Mexico, the Mexican people should be doing so well by now economically that we should need to offer (incentive) rewards for Mexican workers to come across the border to work.

Let me be perfectly clear the way the United States is handling our relations with our southern neighbors, big business partnering with Washington is doing all they can to keep developing economies in a holding pattern, and at the same time, Washington is contributing to the economic decline of American workers and our country's ability to pay its bills. It is the sorriest mess of political mismanagement imaginable. This will become clearer as we discuss various elements that, when brought together, show who not only really runs not just our country but also impacts peoples worldwide. I haven't called our form of governance corporate communism for nothing!

Are American's unwilling to work in the food industry, mining, textile, or any other? I can visualize some of you nodding your heads in the affirmative. Yes, many Americans are unwilling to do some jobs. The way to interest any people in these areas is to raise the pay. We all know the next line. The employers will say they will go out of business. I don't disagree.

In 2008 the price of gas in Mateo California was reported at over $5.00 per gallon and Californians adapted to it. Human nature tells us that we can deal with hardship for a time however; Sooner or later American ingenuity and spirit will prevail in finding a just means to an unjust circumstance.

As Ross Perot said about competing with Mexican wages, in his folksy manner of speaking, "You cain't compete against that." Corporate America knew full well what they were leading our politicians into on the NAFTA deal, and they were just frothing at the mouth until that deal went into effect.

Make no mistake about it, Congress was the responsible entity to craft trade policies that were good for America and the American economy. However, it is as clear as a cloudless sunny day that the goal was to make trade easier and ensure Profitability. It is that simple. Going back more than three to four decades when import or export was getting a footing Congress failed miserably to act in protecting our national interests and security.

They were lined up in goose step, promising that there would be thousands of high-paying jobs as a result of the NAFTA agreement. Well, that turned out to be an outright lie. I guess you could call it another Bay of Pigs. Bill Clinton signed the agreement on December 8, 1993, and it went into effect on January 1, 1994. The partners involved are the United States, Canada, and Mexico.

From the inception, many wondered how well it would work, seeing that the United States and Canada, being developed, would fare out with underdeveloped Mexico in the mix. Further on, I have documented statistical numbers that are eye openers as to how US corporations are working the rich against the poor and the only winners are the investors.

Years of experience under free-trade agreements display a fatalistically flawed idea that older industrialized nations with higher living standards were being required by multinational corporations to lower their standards in order to compete with developing nations. There is only one known outcome in this situation: the corporations will prosper, and the middle class will become the poor working class.

Our elected officials failed to act in a reciprocal manner in requiring corporations that were intent on exporting jobs and wealth to also export prosperity to their impoverished business recipients, comparable to American wages or pay a field leveling tariff on imports, to ward off excessive trade deficits.

However, they have taken advantage of paying the impoverished (that which they were accustomed to). Also, they met environmental and local laws of those backward nations, which were and remain substandard by comparison to those of the US. Swiss banks and the creation of subsidiaries were great tax shields to take many from corporate America to a higher status known as multinational.

George W. Bush said that the UAW had to accept readjustment in the form of lower wages and benefit concessions before the American people would bail out General Motors. Ken Lowenza, president of the Canadian Auto Workers Union, said, "It is absolutely clear that George Bush and his

friends in the Republican Party are trying to punish organized labor, drive down wages, and destroy the middle class."

Whatever Happened to Sherman Antitrust on Monopolies?

The Sherman Antitrust Law was intended to limit the
size of businesses so that they could not monopolize their
sector of business or become dictatorial in business, thereby
controlling market prices. "Too big to fail" is a term that
characterizes twenty-first-century business models quite
well. This brings up the question of what part we the people
should play in whether taxpayer money should be used to
bail them out or, more aptly, break them up?

Seeing that corporations love to tout free markets and
decry regulation, they should be required to live by the same
rules as anyone else. When they make bad investments or
are incompetently managed, they should pay the free-market
price. Sell off parts of their business to ward off bankruptcy,
borrow money on the open market to shore up the business
while they right wrong management decisions, etc., etc.

This would more aptly describe free-market capitalism,
a principle that they tout but overlook when they want we
the people to bail them out when they become too big to be
allowed to fail, because their failure would cause a hardship
on society.

If we were to initiate ethical, social, and moral values to the correct and effective use of available resources, I wonder if the multinational corporations could even begin to adapt to this standard of operating values. Let me define what an economy is again. Not only does an economy consist of production and distribution in a particular geographic region, but also, it consists of the *correct and effective use* of available resources.

Those available resources consists of gathering materials in an ecological manner as possible. That means not raping the earth in the process, but rather doing the least long-term damage as possible, or leaving the environment in as good or better condition than found. Can we agree that concerns for earth, water, air, etc., would be construed as correct?

Effective. An economy is supposed to produce an appropriate level of financial reward (equality) for all the participants, enabling them to be self-reliant and become contributing societal members empowered to support and build societal infrastructure. Can we determine that to mean to be able to contribute to humanitarian needs such as housing, health care systems, education clean water, air, sanitation, transportation, etc.?

Yes, it allows for profits and salaries for CEOs commensurate with responsibilities. *Correct* and *effective* have a very broad and comprehensive meaning. Societies do not do this on Twinkies! It seems that the biggest challenge is to educate corporate executives and investors that they are no more important than those who work under them.

I have developed a phrase for what I determined a worker in the USA needs to make per hour to be financially self-sufficient. To be *financially sufficient for societal integration*, a US worker needs to earn at least $20 per hour. That is to be totally self-supporting and, in a manner of speaking, pay their own way. This would not mean that they are doing extremely well but rather they are only able to go from dependent to independent paying their way.

Was Washington's decision to rescue GM, bail out Fannie Mae, Freddie Mac, AIG, and Citi a good management decision or merely political pandering at the expense of the American people? Many have said, "Look at how well GM has bounced back." I am inclined to believe that they got themselves in a position that warranted their takeover by someone else who has a better business track record. I am inclined to hold their feet to the fire; after all, it is they who fly the free-enterprise banner.

Should they have been compelled to walk the walk in the same manner as they talk the talk? Would someone deserving have taken over GM without a dime of US taxpayer monies spent, lost in the shuffle, or wasted?

Ahead I have covered a couple of examples of US manufacturing plant closures of Carrier Corporation. It states, "The company planned to leave behind a reduced workforce of 1,600 people employed in marketing, sales, product support, warehousing engineering, and research." In other words, they left behind a residual business.

The Carrier Corporation historically has been based in Syracuse, New York, where Willis Carrier moved his facilities from New Jersey in the 1930s. During the late twentieth century, when it was acquired by UTC, United Technologies Corp., it was Central New York State's largest manufacturer.

Due to increasing labor and union costs in the Central New York area, Carrier has substantially downsized its presence in Syracuse, with manufacturing work being moved to a variety of domestic and international locations. Meanwhile, managerial employees were relocated closer to UTC's Connecticut corporate headquarters. This has been a challenge for the Syracuse regional economy.

When every other large corporation follows this same operational policy, eventually they will have less need for home based warehousing, sales, product support, and maybe research. When this same business model is adopted by every other business fleeing to greener pastures, eventually there will be very few American workers left who make enough money to purchase Carrier products or any other, unless the product prices coming back as imports are cheaper and in line with the new lower standard of living in America.

Folks, that's what happens when big business creates de-capitalization and a deflationary economy. I didn't even mention the loss in tax revenue that our federal, state, municipalities, etc., will have to go without.

Without. That is key to this whole tsunami effect. The money is not there to fix the roads and bridges and pay the public employees *that which they have become accustomed to.* The economic chaos and anarchy that is created by such poor oversight deserves a label, don't you think?

Although I picked Carrier Corporation out of the hat, I discovered that Carrier is merely a subsidiary of United Technologies, but theirs is the same story told over and over as hundreds became tens of thousands, eventually tallying into the millions of workers from high-paying product-producing jobs swept away by the cascading evolutionary concept of outsourcing.

Where were our Washington bureaucrats as our trade deficits began to reach such levels that it is a threat to our national security? They have been working at helping corporate America increase free trade. What that means is they have been busy opening the floodgates for corporate American imports and doing nothing to insist on those same enterprises level the playing field by way of import fees in creating a balanced trade concept.

Their free-market capitalistic concept is similar to a surfboarder riding a high wave for as long as it lasts. That is precisely what corporate America is doing: riding the wave for as long as they can, and the very people that we the people put in office to look out for our interests are ignoring their primary responsibility.

Let me be perfectly clear once again. It is the responsibility of the United States Congress to manage) international trade, thereby protecting our workers and homeland security interests. Does this incompetent management jeopardize our national security? You bet it does! They know it, yet they ignore it.

Imperfect Partners is a collage of condensed historical, political, social, and cultural events that contributed to the evolutionary changes that characterizes America's humble beginning, eventually achieving economic stardom, and, finally, as an aging Broadway performer who can only embrace distant memories. The American worker seems only able to sit in the theater and watch others take the spotlight, others who seemingly are less talented than we recall ourselves being.

The commentary for *Imperfect Partners* is the author's opinion, observation, and experience. As much factual research is incorporated and supporting data quoted "What the record shows" will often appear, and I have borrowed from the great news commentator Paul Harvey, famous for his final line, "And that's the rest of the story."

"Hello, Americans, this Is Paul Harvey."

And with those words, ABC News legend Paul Harvey begins another broadcast.

Paul Harvey is the most well-known newsman in the world. He established the gold standard for news and commentary over fifty years ago with his morning and noon News & Comment and his tantalizing broadcast, *The Rest of the Story.*

Born on September 4, 1918, Paul Harvey passed away on February 31, 2009.

The Rest of the Story

It is this author's opinion that Americans in general have become anxious. They are anxious not only about their personal, near-term, and long-term security but also (maybe for the first time in America's history) about the near term and future of where our country as a whole is headed, because, as so goes the country, so goes the status of "We the people."

We are getting to a point where self-concern is less meaningful and concern for all of society is more important, because the increasing ideal of what affects one affects all is looming from the four corners of the earth.

"We the People"

We the people of the USA are a part of the whole.

There are usually two sides to every story. Most of us are familiar with "How big was that fish you caught?" That is one side of the story, and then when the fish is actually weighed and measured, that is the other side of the story. As Paul Harvey would say, "And that's the rest of the story." *Imperfect Partners* is intended to present the rest of the untold story, utilizing the weigh and measure system. What does the record show?

It was predicted more than fifty years ago that America would evolve from a manufacturing-based economy to a services-dominated economy. Frankly, I at least half-believe that the expectations at the time was that automation and technology and invention would replace much production done by human hand, which, in part, turned out to be the case, but I don't think that those early forecasters had an inkling that America's middle class would be left behind. Could those forecasters comprehend what we would have left as, Carrier Corp. reported, "We will retain a residual work force"?

If we knew it was coming, why were we so unprepared to effectively make a smoother transition? The answer is easy enough to see, but I think everyone should follow the evolutionary and created events to draw conclusions from their own observations. Many have heard of the science project of putting a frog in a pan of cold water and slowly turning up the heat. It is said the frog did not realize what was happening until it was too late for it to hop out of the pan. Metaphorically, it could be said that this is an analogy of what happened to America's industrial might.

Americans have always accepted the premise that to the victor belongs the spoils of the game. It is the way capitalism is supposed to work, strictly supply and demand. The strong survive and the weak fade away. Americans have a history of loving their sports and readily accept that one team wins and the other loses. American workers accepted the hand dealt them as fate that dealt an unavoidable economic fatal blow, and they just happen to be in the wrong place at the wrong time.

Obviously, when corporate America says free-market capitalism is the premium system around the globe, they are doing it tongue in cheek. If our system is capitalistic the corporations should have a minimum of need for maintaining the close relationships with Washington and vice versa. Folks, there is no such thing as free-market capitalism when you get right down to how corporate America is working the crowd. If we the people regarded our Washington bureaucrats as a business, we would be forced to recognize that their best customer base is the corporations.

US taxpayers vote them into office, pay their salaries, and expect unbiased results from their leadership. On the other hand, or the rest of the story is that lobbyists give them their bonuses and get the better or best results. This works out to corruption at worst, and a case of imperfect partners at best.

> "No servant can serve two masters: for either he will hate the one, and love the other; or else he will hold to the one, and despise the other. Ye cannot serve God and mammon. No servant can serve two masters, since either he will hate one and love the other." (Luke 16:13)

Our elected servants have taken an oath of office to work impartially for all the people all the time, rather than cave in to tips and bonuses from special interests willing to pay for favors. What does this tell us about the relationship between lobbyists and congressmen or congresswomen becoming millionaires while in office? It amazes me that our justice system does not prosecute pay for play wherever it can be proven.

Furthermore, the emphasis of almost the entire content of this book concerning such things as the demise of the middle class, the selling of America's economy, incompetence of leadership, etc., etc., is hinged on the concept that we the people are governed by an entrenched reactionary system that the author describes at best: imperfect partners!

To Tell the Truth—Just Not All the Truth

When state departments release economic statistics, it gives the appearance that significant economically developing countries in the crusade against poverty are dramatically improving. They will cite great strides in GDP and GNP. One of their favorites is the economic growth of Mexico since the ratification of NAFTA.

Don't be too quick to give it up and applaud about the gross domestic product (GDP), gross national product (GNP), and other economic indices. Reports allege significant increases in what appears wealth for the citizenry of emerging countries.

With Mexico as our benchmark, the reports and the fantastic state department claims sound and look impressive, but the status of the people has not changed much. Except that the rich have gotten richer—much richer. One sincere question will answer how well prosperity is being exported to Mexico's people since NAFTA: why do so many Mexicans want to immigrate to the United States?

GDP is the market value of everything produced within a country. GNP is the value of what's produced by a country's residents, no matter where they live.

It is easy to understand who is taking an economic whipping by comparing GNP, the standard of living, and immigration from our southern border. Not only is the good ole USA taking it on the nose, but also Mexican workers under the NAFTA agreement are taking a shellacking at the same time.

CNIME (Spanish: National Council of Maquiladora Export Industries) said that the average maquiladora wage is 70 pesos per day ($8.50). Many Mexicans complain that although maquiladoras produce jobs, in thirty years, they have produced very few homegrown spin-off industries or entrepreneurs. So much for raising emerging economies out of poverty with the help of American investors!

Note: Homegrown spin-off industries would be a different story when it comes to American investment in China. China will teach us a lesson we will never forget.

As I promised you early on in my report, we would take a look where our economy has gone, following NAFTA.

The number of facilities owned by all other countries combined number 2,731 while the United States' *alone* is 1683.

Mexico's Gross Domestic Product (GDP) in purchasing power parity (PPP) was estimated at US $1.353 trillion in 2006 and $886.4 billion in nominal exchange rates.[4] As such, its standard of living, as measured in GDP in PPP per capita, was US $12,500. The World Bank reported in 2007 that the country's Gross National Income in market exchange rates was the second highest in Latin America, after Brazil, at US $820.319 billion,[16] which lead to the highest income per capita in the region at $7,830.[17] As such, Mexico is now firmly established as an upper middle-income country. After the slowdown of 2001, the country has recovered and has grown 4.2, 3.0, and 4.8 percent in 2004, 2005 and 2006,[18] even though it is considered to be well below Mexico's potential growth.[14]

Are you impressed with the (numbers) in this report? One would be led to believe that Mexico should be sending aid to the United States. Let's look at another economic indice that may explain "the rest of the story."

Mexican trade is fully integrated with that of its North American partners: close to 90 percent of Mexican exports and 50 percent of its imports are traded with the United States and Canada.

Export partners	US 90.9%, Canada 2.2%, Spain 1.4%, Germany 1.3%, Colombia 0.9% (2006)
Import partners	US 53.4%, China 8%, Japan 5.9% (2005)

Close to 90% of its exports go to the United States while only 2.2% go to Canada. This data tells us that Canada must be protecting its national interests, while the USA apparently is listening to the sucking sound that Ross Perot talked about, as American jobs went to our southern border.

Corporate America has been producing products in Mexico and shipping it back to the USA for a handsome profit: 53.4% of Mexico's imports come from the USA. You can be assured that much of these imports are materials for fabrication or assembly purposes. The question is who is getting rich from this (venture)? The corporations, of course! The Mexican workers are not, and we know what has happened to American jobs and wealth.

Where is Washington on this dilemma when we the people need them? Help must still be on the way, but I think everyone who has been looking for it has given up hope long ago. The Bay of Pigs syndrome! This is a good look at corporate communism working at capacity: They have the (authorization) NAFTA signed, sealed, and delivered, thanks to US leadership. There is still more to come; America is up for sale. Bill Clinton will give China MFN status followed by their induction into the WTO.

President Clinton, President Bush, President Carter, President Ford, and Vice President Gore—all these presidents endorsed NAFTA.

GATT (General Agreement on Tariffs and Trade) and the WTO are like Siamese twins; they are inseparable.

GATT/WTO

According to its preamble, the purpose of the GATT is the "substantial reduction of tariffs and (other) trade barriers and the elimination of preferences, on a reciprocal and mutually advantageous basis."

53k - 8 sec @ 56k

www.law.duke.edu/lib/researchguides/gatt.html

www.law.duke.edu/lib/researchguides/gatt.html · Cached

In other words, GATT removes all the (substantial) obstacles for the corporations to produce cheaply. On top of that, the WTO can enforce the will of the corporations by removing import quotas. Does this also help to explain why 90 percent of Mexico's exports are coming to the United States?

The devil is in the details, stellar statistics are the accumulation of product output, and corporate transactions accounting of business transactions at the national level not only proves little but also distorts real numbers that define how well or how poorly a nation's citizenry is doing economically. If you can imagine on a worldwide basis that the rich are getting richer and the poor poorer, can you imagine how that divide is ramping up in Mexico?

What does add up is the billions and trillions of profits being made and distributed among the top 2 percent of the world's population (investors).

The Powerfully Rich and the Politically Empowered

It is the relationship of these two factions that is a hot topic of American conversation and controversy, from coffee sippers to car poolers, grocery store shoppers, and extending to what is left of Union member meetings.

There is no existing earthly entity that can make sweeping changes take place as quickly, or cause change to come so slowly, as the will of those with wealth and those with political clout to decide.

The rich and powerful, who had the means to control, have engineered and legislated ways and means to make the systems work according to their will for selective advantage, and they wasted no time in getting the job done.

Capitalism is as old as the United States of America itself. Those who saw opportunity most certainly seem to have noticed that economic evolution could be channeled with their creative molding.

The Dinosaur Met a Swift Demise

Throughout America can still be seen vestiges of a former era and socio-economic culture in the form of window-less warehouses, boarded-up buildings, and grass and weeds growing up through cracks in the concrete of factory parking lots no longer used, as a testament to an empire that once stood. While this sounds like a descriptive exaggeration of what many attribute to market trends, the new global economy or the result of natural attrition, the evidence in the artifacts indeed declares some cataclysmic event did occur.

Is it any wonder how this writer came to the conclusion that what happened, coupled with *how* it happened, to the American worker is nothing short of political and economic terrorism?

In other places around the globe, we hear of millions of people being uprooted from their homes, immigrating to safer places because of warring factions creating imminent danger to their life and property. What we have experienced right here in countless communities over a thirty-plus-year period was workers being uprooted because of closed-down industries. Their only choice was to move on and try to reestablish a new life in other places.

In other words, we had what could be described as internal immigration of Americans attempting not to better their lot in life but to merely survive economically. There would be nothing unacceptable about corporations closing facilities for economic downturns, restructuring, management error, etc.

But much of this was not the case. It, simply put, was a case of partnering with American leadership to do business in a foreign nation. When you take a close look at the economic situation and plight of those unfortunate millions who experienced that Holocaust and understand the total negligent incompetence of our lawmakers, in how they simply nodded their heads to the corporate bosses, I don't think the term "war on the middle class" is as accurate a description as "political and economic terrorism."

Could such economic, social, and emotional anarchy have been prevented? Could safeguards have been emplaced to protect those impacted by elimination? The fact after the fact is now viewable as nothing was done to prepare for a mutually beneficial transition from a manufacturing to a services economy. Leadership proved to not be very good at planning for the future but rather proved to be in a sense reactionary to a crisis.

An economy cannot be sustained on public service jobs alone, insurance companies, advertising and selling subscriptions to telephone, Internet, and TV services. The services industry, which can be hot for those in the business, still represents red-ink liability against inventory, sales, and profits. They play the similar part as popcorn sold at a theater performance sell out. It doesn't sustain the performance or make it any worse or better, it only gives an extra comfort and convenience to the theater-going customer.

Let's be honest, all the peripheral businesses (i.e., tech and energy) are indeed essential and usually exist because of the core. Our Washington bureaucrats will all attest to the fact that a nation that does not possess a manufacturing base is treading on thin ice concerning national security. I don't understand how one after another can proclaim that statement and they still gave the farm away.

Our Forefathers Were Indeed Pioneers:

Not only did American workers mine the ore, fire the furnaces, make the steel, and roll automobiles, refrigerators, air conditioners, and thousands of other long-forgotten "Made in USA" products off the assembly lines, American workers were also our own best customers.

The USA was the economic, social, and cultural tough act for the rest of the world to follow. As progressive as this all sounds and appears, it was not an easy row to hoe for the struggling American workforce. Those who were a part of the startup when trickle-down economics could and did work, those workers in that generation had to fight for every inch of economic ground gained, and they had aching backs, sweaty brows, leathered hands, and the scars to prove it.

For the struggles of organized labor in the early years, it was not uncommon for violence to erupt between striking workers and management security guards reinforced with local police agencies with injuries and fatalities taking place in the contest of wills. Labors' struggle to pass on to subsequent generations a standard of living that many think was the result of merely being an American does not do justice to perseverance through hell and high water that our ancestry endured to give their posterity something better than they had. They were the (budding) new middle class.

The Industrial Revolution Sets Sail

They did not give up the fight that started as early as the late 1800s, and by the 1960s, unions were losing their ability to look out for worker interests as manufacturers moved operations off shore. By the closing end of the 1960s, you could tell that the US industrial ship was no longer anchored as you could feel the adrift of this mighty vessel.

Metaphorically and literally speaking, manufacturers were pulling the levers to the electric main panels to the OFF position, unbolting the machines from the floor, padlocking the doors, and loading ships with the machinery to do business elsewhere. Labor would begin to live on their laurels; the theater cast was being made up with new actors at less pay to perform and pass more revenue to the sponsors.

At America's industrial zenith, (80 percent) of the consumer products carried US union labels. Unionization was the catalyst that propelled the standard of living for millions of Americans to the highest in the world. Was it any wonder that America stood as a shining beacon on a hill in the eyes of the world?

The Struggle Is Far from Over, and Not Just for Americans

As late as the 1990s, after Bill Clinton signed the NAFTA agreement, with the maquiladoras locating over the border in mass numbers, Mexican workers attempted to organize labor. Some of those attempts met the same resistance as early unions in the USA.

Do Those Things Still Happen in the Twenty-First Century?

There are documented reports that some Mexican organizers were killed while trying to unite North American Free Trade Agreement (NAFTA) workers; subsequently, the corporations nipped in the bud any attempts of Mexican workers to follow the pattern that gave rise of the middle class in the USA. So much for their promise of high-paying jobs for America's endorsement of the NAFTA agreement.

If you are wondering if it is possible for people to be murdered just because they attempt to organize labor in our sophisticated world, the answer is yes. In Mexico and many other so-called emerging markets, it happened as recent as after 1994.

Not only that, but also pregnant Mexican women have been subjected to high levels of carcinogenic materials in the maquiladoras, child labor was becoming rampant in many regions, and at the heart of these occurrences was American investment. It really has been an opportunity for investors!

If you were wondering why I said a little earlier that the multinational corporations were introducing prosperity to undeveloped nations, at the slowest rate possible. This is just the tip of the iceberg.

It is difficult to talk about the rising up of the middle class without recognizing unions for the achievement, but because of the added costs to corporate America (labor cost, environmental laws, and taxes), timing and foreign nations hungry to be become a part of the industrialized world would deliver results similar to a killer frost settling into the orchards before the fruit is picked. If nothing else, for American labor, a long, tough winter lies ahead.

Are our environmental laws a good reason or a good excuse for American corporations exporting wealth and jobs? Not if earth, water, and air pollution are less important in foreign lands. Global trade should incorporate universal standards of operations to be met. This is a sound way of protecting the environment in a global sense. Even this is not going far enough to create fair trade, worker rights, equality, and prosperity for all. As I have mentioned, import tariffs are a necessity to level the playing field and encourage manufacturers to reconsider (point of production and point of use).

If we held our competition to our own human rights or abuses and environmental standards, etc., we probably would not be doing much business with China, and Bill Clinton giving China most-favored nation (MFN) trade status (1994) would not have been possible and would never have taken place. You cannot have two sets of rules for those playing the same game and call it fair trade, free trade, or a level playing field.

If you are wondering about our disastrous trade deficit, hold on to your hat, we will be looking at that.

The top brass from GM said, "Their inability to compete with foreign auto producers costs them $1700. per vehicle that foreign producers did not have to incur.

It is virtually impossible to achieve world-class values in any area—be it environment, product quality, social values that incorporate financial security, health care, etc., for workers—without uniform global standards of operations. I don't expect all my readers to get what I am proposing within the scope of uniform standard by talking about it only one time. Therefore, you can expect to hear of this concept as we discuss it using different illustrations in implementation and effect. Bear with me.

Several European nations are still just as unionized as the USA formerly used to be, but with the new modern high-speed mobility of manufacturers, organizing workers at transplant facilities has been largely ineffective against powerful anti-union forces. Coupled with mobility, most multi-nationals now possess a portfolio of locations from which to choose for production and distribution.

Remember, the maquiladoras are not called twin plants for nothing. The power of unions has declined to the point of extinction in most Old World manufacturing regions. Manufacturers will move operations when and where they can exercise complete freedom to maximize profits and minimize moral, environmental, and ethical commitment to their host nation, domestic law, or regard for the citizenry.

What was created to help them achieve their ends and overcome all obstacles in their way? The WTO, of course. If you were thinking the WTO is looking out for workers and consumers, think again.

When you understand what groups make up the WTO and whose interest they represent, you probably will have little problem understanding why I have made the assertion that the global economy is largely governed by corporate communism. It is a generally known and accepted saying that whoever controls the money controls the world. That being said, begin to think about it in the following manner: who has the most control over not only our economy but also *all* economies?

It is easily seen what the calling card is for the corporations looking to strike it rich by exporting jobs from wealthier nations to nations that have weak or no environmental standards and nonexistent labor standards. When George W. Bush was working on the plan to bail out GM, the first mandate he issued was that the union workers would have to take concessions.

The political approach to leveling the playing field to compete with foreign nations has always been about lowering the wages for Americans and avoiding boosting foreign workers' wages and/or implementing tariffs. Congress refusal to implement tariffs has been one of the greater gifts to manufacturers, foreign and domestic alike. What does this say for understanding the saying "The rich are getting richer, and the poor are getting poorer"? The result is fewer American jobs and foreign workers working under status quo.

Any time and any way we look at our international trade situation and how it is carried on, we can only come to one conclusion: the corporations rule, and the US Congress can be seen nodding their heads in agreement to whatever the corporations need to make trade easier and more profitable.

By the time you have finished reading this book, you will have an understanding of the phrase "global economy." You will be able to discuss the issues with friends and relatives rather than merely nod your head in agreement to their rant.

The term "nodding our head" is something I have used commonly throughout *Imperfect Partners* that stems from a joke I once heard. It goes like this: Two people are preparing to drive a fence post. One person is holding the post and says to the second person holding the hammer, "When I nod my head, you hit it!"

The moral of the story is that you want to be sure that when you nod your head signifying agreement or acknowledgment, your communication is made clear and understandable.

The big threes UAW and the steel industry are prime examples of the art of deflating the value of labor in America. Long before the auto sector began to take big hits, the steel, textile, rubber, aluminum, paper, etc., and almost any basic building materials production was on the skids to finished products made elsewhere. Even select mined minerals was dropping, and in a time of increased consumption.

Why was this so? Lax regulation, environmental laws, human rights, etc., and the failure of the US Congress to implement any form of fair trade policy. Let us be reminded it is the responsibility of our Congress to manage international commerce folks. They were not doing their job, period.

Civil servants may have thought it would not reach them.

Public Employee Pay Gains Outpace Private Sector

February 2000. There is a widening gap between the total compensation (pay and benefits) of state or local government workers and private-sector employees, according to a recent article "State, local government workers see pay gains" in USA Today. This conclusion is based on an analysis of data reported by the Bureau of Labor Statistics (2008).

The data show that the gap has been widening every year, rising by an average of $1.02 an hour last year and $2.45 an hour over the past three years. The article points out that benefits are a big factor in the growing gap, as private sector companies have trimmed pension benefits and asked employees to pay a greater share of medical costs, while few government-run public services have imposed similar restraints.

There are two factors in play that have been developing not just since 2008, as this report indicates. The reluctance for governmental agencies to make necessary cuts to balance their budgets goes all the way back to the early 1970s. That is when the public sector began to pull ahead of private sector workers.

The one important thing to remember is that in the beginning it just was not as (fiscally) noticeable until more recent times (2008). By 2008 it had reached crisis mode. If you are wondering how this author knows this to be true, I was there. I am a casualty of what a few journalists since around the year 2000 called "war on the middle class." I experienced superior fringe benefits being slashed and pay raises being halted or rebundled at contract negotiations in ways that were concessionary. Mind you, this was not a one-time event but a repetitive event, with each ensuing contract period beginning in 1974. That's twenty-five years of decline. At the same time, every public services organizations that I am familiar with were able to receive incremental yearly increases.

Why were state and local governments reluctant to make adjustments when economic decline began to gain a foothold? You guessed it. They are elected, and a very large segment of their constituency are police/security/public services/teachers/health/municipal/transportation, etc., etc. You get the picture; the list is long, and civil servants vote.

I am very familiar with what really took place. I am most familiar with disparities between public- and private-sector employees up to the state level, NYS in particular. Further on, we will discuss what happened between public- and private-sector workers in New Jersey.

As their budget dilemma seems to mimic all states, the similarities are the same. Every state has befell the same problem and for the identical reason. What does this have to do with the new global economy? At a time when the public-sector workers should have been undergoing give backs to keep in step with what private sector workers were subject to, they continued with increases as if nothing had changed. Service workers represent a formidable task force, and elected office holders who decide their benefits packages knew it was within their best interest to buy the workers' loyalty if they were to count on reelection.

For years prior to the 1960s, many public-service workers were not unionized with wages or salaries and benefits being determined by their locality's legislative process, be it village, town, county, state, or up to the federal level. Here is the turning point.

The UAW was one of the strongest unions in the nation, and Detroit was booming. The auto companies often gave union workers what they wanted rather than face a prolonged production shutdown. Let's remember though, the good times would not last forever. Private-sector skilled and unskilled workers across the board usually made more money than public-sector workers during that time.

Public-service workers usually were paid less but had better benefits such as early retirement, personal days, vacation time, and health care coverage. Producing a product versus rendering service has some unique differences that determine how much time is required on the job being productive. You may look at it in this manner: a civil servant could usually take a longer coffee break than a factory worker without showing a loss of productivity.

In spite of the need to compensate civil servants according to an austerity-based budget, leaders continued to hand out raises and benefits that they could not afford. They could not afford to, but they kept handing out increases to ensure voter loyalty.

Hence, it became well known that the best jobs were to be had in public services. We must remember, private-sector jobs were shrinking dramatically at the same time public-service jobs were expanding markedly. This practice by public leaders just to appease civil servants would go on until it went into crisis mode.

The vary people who could have saved America by managing and balancing domestic spending to the level of incoming resources continued to do what they are best known for: spending money that they no longer had coming into the coffers from tax revenues mainly from lost industries vanishing.

It couldn't be easier to see that we are governed by reactionary leaders. Reactionary, in this case, is to indicate leadership that displays no future plan and only reacts to crises that come their way. The old guard that refuses to change or adapt. It was leadership at every level right up to the White House that contributed to becoming a society living on borrowed money and borrowed time.

Public service employees held a valuable wild card. Most service jobs were not exportable, and their power united in numbers to threaten legislators with being ousted from office at the ballot box continues to be their ace in the hole. But with high-speed communications, things are changing and changing faster than ever. Many services jobs are indeed becoming threatened with exportability.

What do I mean by exporting prosperity as a means to help our own economic standing? Look at it this way. There was a time when much of what we Americans bought was imported from Japan. Following WWII, it was called the rebuilding of Japan. After about twenty-five years of heavy imports from Japan, the Japanese standard of living came up to our own. Japanese labor was no longer a cash cow, and corporate America moved on.

Now the new feeding ground became China and Mexico, among lesser places. The moral of the story is that as each nation moves up to become comparable to our economic standard, the issues of trade imbalance mostly disappear. This is why our congresses should openly recognize their responsibility to implement (early) intervention and put American workers first. Ultimately it benefits foreign workers at the same time in terms of leveling the playing field.

This is the sorriest mess of incompetence I can imagine. Our trade imbalances with China and Mexico can easily and quickly be solved. All it takes is the right intervention, and the quicker, the better—period.

During those decades of corporate America's nation galloping, the UAW held on to more of their wages and benefits longer than a lot of other industrial workers, but it would be only a matter of time until they too would be hit, and hit hard.

By autumn of 2008, not only did the UAW take concessions (again) in their 2007 contract, but also because of the impending doom of the automotive market, they were facing the knockout punch. It is a picture that is exactly what corporations have been working toward—that is, to drive American wages to the lowest common denominator.

American corporations can take all the credit for ultimately creating the global economic environment where, at last, American labor has been forced to compete with some of the lower-paid workers in their industry (segment). This is how companies like Toyota, Honda, and BMW are now willing to transplant facilities in the good ole US of A.

What in the world are international organizations like the UN, WTO, ILO doing to fulfill their role for we the people of the world? Member nations hold in their hand, documentation of commitment to look out for the interest of their citizenry in general and worker rights, and/or abuses, specifically in the new global economy. Not only are they doing nothing, but also there are documented instances of counterproductive sabotage for preventing engagement in the process.

Later, we will explore "WTO (World Trade Organization) snubs ILO (International Labor Organization." It is a royal eye opener as to what disgraceful disregard the leaders of most of these member nations have for their own people when the represented industries called the meeting to order (in a sense).

I have promised you that we will review the WTO, ILO, and the IMF—we will get to it.

Every president of the United States of America says his job is to protect the American people. The question is, have they become desensitized from what it means to protect? Is their distractions with serving corporate America so intent that they think we the people no longer notice? It is written, "No one can serve two masters, because he either will hate one and love the other or be loyal to one and despise the other."

What Is a Linchpin?

Linchpin:
1. A locking pin inserted in the end of a shaft, as in an axle, to prevent a wheel from slipping off.
2. A central cohesive element
3. Dictionary.com

Competent management, or good management, is one of the main linchpins that hold the wheels of our systems integrity from slipping off.

There are countless ways and means to illustrate what has become of the American middle class. To say those who are responsible for checking the linchpins is about as accurate of a description as one can get.

The wheels of the American economy have definitely been allowed to slip off.

Keep in mind as you read this book—we will be reviewing the record of such organizations as our own Department of Labor, the WTO, UN, ILO, EFCA (Employee Free Choice Act), MFN (most favored nation), and much more.

What part have these agencies or policies contributed to wreaking havoc on workers?

We may not all agree on all issues, but we will all understand the basic things that affect all of us a little better if we consider what the record of the very agencies that were created to advance world economy shows.

A Life Cycle Comes to an End

By the 1980, with job security becoming so unpredictable, more and more Americans sought self-employment as entrepreneurs, independent tech support services, and even going so far as returning to a simpler lifestyle began increasing, and the trend is growing. The life cycle of dependable long-term employment with the good-benefits security blanket that Chester Riley enjoyed was about to come to an end, and "Peg, I'm home" would merely be an echo from the past.

Business journals are predicting that with corporations looking to escape the high cost of health care, doing away with company pensions, and other added cost benefits, we will be seeing more and more subcontracted workers who will be going to the office as usual. The only difference is that they will be self-employed, possibly working for many clients, completing projects on a temporary basis, and paying for their own benefits.

Another Time and Place

Walter Philip Reuther (September 1, 1907–May 9, 1970) was an American labor union leader who made the United Automobile Workers a major force.

Reuther was possibly the most influential labor leader ever in American history.

When monopolies jeopardize the safety of the country, they can no longer be trusted in private hands to use them for a profit.

That is my private philosophy. So stated Walker Reuther.

For a Twenty-Year Period, Economic Prosperity Was for All

When one segment of our economy as big as the UAW was—sets the tone for advancing labor's position it significantly influences others to follow suite.

Also on the front lines was James "Jimmy" Hoffa. Hoffa fought as relentlessly for the Teamsters union as Reuther did for the UAW, raising wages, improving working conditions and long-term financial security for union families.

Although those were contentious times, employer and worker prospered alike. It may be said these two men led the movement that changed the status of millions or workers; American manufacturing and transportation, two of the biggest enterprises on the continent, truly America was a middle-class dominated society.

Does the rise of a vibrant middle class explain why America made such a surge—a boom, in fact—in building infrastructure following World War II for a twenty-year period? I think it does.

True Freedom Fighters Do Not Fare Well in America

Reuther died in a plane crash that has perplexed those who have thoroughly investigated the suspicious crash for years.

Reuther stood beside Martin Luther King Jr. while he made the "I Have a Dream" speech, during the 1963 March on Washington. In October 1968, a year and a half before the fatal crash, he and his brother Victor were almost killed in a small private plane as it approached Dulles Airport. Both incidents are amazingly similar; the altimeter in the fatal crash was believed to have malfunctioned.

When Victor Reuther was interviewed many years after the fatal crash, he said, "I and other family members are convinced that both the fatal crash and the near-fatal one in 1968 were not accidental."

Walter Philip Reuther (September 1, 1907–May 9, 1970).

Shortly after World War II until the Last Half of the Sixties

America was in a new growth spurt similar to infrastructure puberty. New money, where did it come from? It was the result of a thriving middle class able to carry the tax burden for infrastructure.

And with the Flow of Wealth

Government spending expanded greatly in areas of infrastructure. National transportation system expanded networks like never before, or since. There was what could be described as new money availability. With a thriving middle class, social programs could be funded to meet social needs never supported before.

This new money brought educational opportunity to the mentally and physically challenged (the passed over). New money was responsible for making a college education attainable by anyone with a desire to learn and excel, rather than just the privileged and wealthy.

New money was responsible for raising our baseline standard of living, social security benefits were beefed up, and a good thing they were, for today it makes up most of many Americans' golden year's income. And all for some, with corporate America's reneging, underfunding, no funding, etc., of pension funds, it has been a blessing in disguise.

Finally, America was growing a sophisticated middle class amid the aristocrats. More and more people were able to afford conveniences from the latest inventions. They were beginning to vacation—so much so that the tourism industry was expanding to meet the demand for new middle-class luxuries. People were dressing better, eating out, going to the theater, and putting many of the latest conveniences in their own homes.

Refrigeration, One of the World's Most Important Inventions

General Electric Co. (GE) had been developing commercial and household refrigerators for many years, but it wasn't until 1923 that it put substantial resources into developing the home version. Because refrigerators on the market had not yet been perfected, whoever solved some of the early problems could dominate the market.

For one thing, refrigerators had dropped in price but still cost $450 for the most inexpensive model—a great deal of money in a time when most people had annual incomes of less than $2,000. These early compression models used the refrigerants ammonia, sulfur dioxide, or methyl chloride, which could explode and were toxic if leaked. The refrigerators also had a short life because these refrigerants were corrosive.

The first home refrigerators were also noisy and needed servicing every few months. The noisy motor was separate from the cooling box and could be put in the basement or elsewhere, but the separation of the two parts also forced the compressor to work harder to pump the refrigerant to the cooling box in the kitchen.

Considering that government requirements in the 1990s called for refrigerators that would run on less electricity, it is ironic that in the 1920s a compelling reason to pursue compression technology was that it required electricity twenty-four hours a day and would use a lot of power. The use of electricity was in its infancy, but GE was betting that electricity would become more popular than gas.

In 1927, General Electric began marketing the first refrigerator with a hermetically sealed motor and an attached cooling box. It was called the "Monitor Top," because the motor was in a circular box on top of the cooling compartment.

By 1929, the company had sold an astonishing fifty thousand monitor tops. That same year, GE replaced the wood cabinet with steel and brought out its first all-steel refrigerators. In 1931, GE produced its one-millionth Monitor Top refrigerator.

Footnote

The history of the refrigerator is interesting, and as an added bonus, this report also depicts a classic example as to how compatibility between conglomerates partner with one another (i.e., please notice the relationship between General Electric and the utility companies).

Do you suppose the reason for the auto industry to be so sluggish in improving gas mileage, or perfecting electric, or alternative fuels in today's cars is because they are deeply invested in the oil companies and really are not ready to change or do not want change anytime soon?

Could the same be true with our global economy? We have had at least a twenty-year lapse of management that should have ensured a balance of prosperity rather than riches for the capitalists and de-capitalizing middle America. Do you suppose it is moving as fast as those who can make it to move are allowing it to move?

NAFTA was nothing more than embodiment of corporate greed. The economic decline was well underway long before NAFTA (1994), but it goes to show that political leadership either learned absolutely nothing about (managing) free trade, or they were preoccupied with making free trade easier for corporate America.

The Results You Can Expect for Mismanagement

What has less government regulation netted for our country? Wealth never seen before for corporations. When the compensation for CEOs reaches over two hundred times that of average earners, that alone tells a revealing story.

At the same time, we the people are left with the minimum wage (protection), food stamp programs, free-trade promises, and fallacies that they are doing what the American people want. Do you think maybe they know what the people want but are ignoring it because they are working off their debt to the spear carriers of big business bosses? How far must they go before we the people begin to think that just maybe such incompetent leadership amounts to acts of nonviolent terrorism?

There is one thing that Democrats and Republican seem to be unified on; Outsourcing, it just seems to pay well. The question is who is the richer for it?

When you and I expend our resources buying and we sell almost nothing, it will not be long before we become financially ruined, period. What has taken place was just plain disastrous for the American worker, putting our global leadership role in jeopardy and our national security at great risk. If that isn't a form of terrorism, what else can we the people label it? Maybe *stupidity*?

Now for a glimpse of the future forty years ahead.

When it becomes thoroughly understood that a middle class represents an economic threat to the ultra-rich club, it also becomes much easier to answer why there is a "war on the middle class," as it has been labeled in recent times around year 2000.

This is a complex issue, and we will discuss other important aspects to substantiate a systematic corporate world strategy to retain 50 percent of the world's wealth by the top 2 percent of the world's population. When the majority of a population is kept in dependency on government for many of the basics for survival, they also become more under control.

True Reformers (Taken Out)

There is one thread of continuity that follows the true freedom fighters like Reuther, Hoffa, and King. The thread of continuity is this" Reuther and King, with the exception of Hoffa. It is highly likely that Hoffa was part of a power struggle. It is a fairly unanimous belief that these social-justice advocates were killed either directly or indirectly because of posing a threat to corporate America's greed.

European Oligarchy Versus
Corporate Communism

European history is long and has its share of the rich ruling ruthlessly, with little or no regard for the rule of law. People came from around the globe flocking to the shores of the USA with only what they could carry, little or no money, and spoke different languages. But they had hope, determination, and a work ethic that could not be constrained.

It makes us wonder what they would think if they could see how much has changed and how much has come full circle and remains the same. If conditions of ethics, competence, and common sense of treating others as you want others to treat you continue to slip through the cracks, those early immigrants would probably shake their heads and say, "This is the kind of things we thought we escaped from in our old country."

Corporate America has been extremely successful in silently leading from behind the scenes, peddling influence that has gutted the American economy and threatened our national security.

I do realize that there is virtually no one pointing the finger at our own US Congress for nearly a half-century of incompetent leadership while they choose to blame the countries which we import from. That is little more than a ruse to draw attention away from our nation's failure to look out for their own people. Let us not forget, NAFTA was the brain child of corporate America, with the promise of creating thousands of high-paying jobs. This was bought hook, line, and sinker by our White House, going way back to Ronald Reagan.

Excerpt

President Ronald Reagan had broached the idea of a free-trade agreement with Mexico in the 1980s, when trade between the two countries was high volume but in many cases restricted. But nothing ever came of it.

Then a debt crisis in the middle of that decade changed Mexico's mind. "It led Latin America to embrace market-oriented policies and abandon a longtime strategy that had focused on the promotion of local industries," says Cameron.

On top of that, he adds, Mexico's then-president Carlos Salinas de Gortari, who had won the presidency in 1988 in an election some considered fraudulent, had reason to want to show he had earned the job. NAFTA was part of his attempt to "legitimize his presidency by announcing that Mexico is essentially joining the First World by signing a free-trade agreement with the US."

You might say the world was duped by fallacies of those eager to do business with indigent nations.

Powerful forces eager to turn the world upside down in the way commerce had been carried on used government and or created agencies such as the WTO, UN, and others to carry out their agenda that would eventually lead to worldwide economic control. Follow the money and you will know who rules the world.

New World Order
Conspiracy Theory

The new world order, or NWO, is claimed to be an emerging clandestine totalitarian world government by various conspiracy theories. The common theme in conspiracy theories about a new world order is that a secretive power elite with a globalist agenda is conspiring to eventually rule the world through an authoritarian world government, which will replace sovereign nation-states, and an all-encompassing propaganda whose ideology hails the establishment of the new world order as the culmination of history's progress.

Many influential historical and contemporary figures have therefore been alleged to be part of a cabal that operates through many front organizations to orchestrate significant political and financial events, ranging from causing systemic crises to pushing through controversial policies, at both national and international levels, as steps in an ongoing plot to achieve world domination.

Crafting trade deals such as NAFTA, which is a proven disaster, and creating the WTO was an even-worse idea because it transferred much of the powers from national sovereignty into the hands of the WTO. In my research covering all the aspects of the WTO, I could add volumes to this book, but to put a perspective on the overall workings of the WTO, their purpose seems evident that they favor developing nations, and as such, they enact policy and exert control over developing nations, which is just what the multinationals want for huge profits.

When all the smoke clears and the dust settles around NAFTA, the WTO, the International Monetary Fund (IMF), and the United Nations (UN), you are left with only one conclusion: these are all manufactured organization or front organizations used by the multinationals. They act as spear carriers or water boys that take the heat off government's failure to lead and look out for the people, and consequently, this incompetence has led to our very own national security at risk.

The choice is yours, whatever you choose to call it, the new global economy or the new world order.

If you are wondering why I have portrayed all the above organizations and NAFTA with such negative review, hold on, as I will be getting to that further on.

For unknown reasons, Mexico failed to take advantage of what they must have learned from US manufacturers to create homegrown industries of their own. On the other hand, China has been very resourceful in copying, stealing intellectual properties, and, finally, becoming a viable competitor.

Now we must deal with Chinese imports versus American imports (from China). It is beginning to look as though corporate America got a little more than they bargained for with resourceful China. It has been said about a good father to his son: "I taught him all I knew, he must have learned something on his own." And so it is with China.

An Economy Is Defined as Correct and Effective Use of Available Resources

Does that also include our most important resource, people? See Investor words.com below.

Absolute capitalism centers itself with absolute profit. That means that capitalistic investors have been afforded extensive freedoms to move about and use of all available resources, relatively free from any commitment to any given society and loose adherence to the rule of law.

Well, actually, free trade, the WTO, and the IMF make sure that corporations are well protected by overriding poorer nations' domestic rule of law. In other words, they have the power to dictate to whoever gets caught in the global web.

Economy, definition: activities related to the production and distribution of goods and services in a particular geographic region. The correct and effective use of available resources.

Free trade and capitalism: the idealists have spent enormous amounts of energy and capital to indoctrinate society with the premise that free trade and capitalism, in particular, are fundamental cornerstones that define what a democracy is.

I can agree that there is some truth in that; the only thing is that it is not all the truth, in my opinion.

They could use reminding and reeducating on what constitutes an economy. However, they have been successful in convincing we the people that we are lucky to have the best system in the world. Somehow the correct and effective use of available resources has been interpreted by them to apply to profit. These most important principles would ultimately require moral and social implementation.

I wanted to be sure about what I believed defined corporate communism. However, the definition of *communism* seems to lean more toward "common ownership," while I believed *communism* meant "power in the hands of a few."

That is what I meant to convey to my readers. Power in the hands of a few to mean the powerful elite who hold a majority of the world's wealth leading from behind the scenes, pedaling influence money for powerful politicians to use their legislative powers to pave the golden highway for global control of the production of goods, services, and distribution. Hence, corporate communism.

Does it make you wonder if you could find any embarrassment among the United Nations (UN) members, the World Trade Organization (WTO), and others who say they are committed to identical principles as correct and effective use of available resources?

In the retail business, they call this tactic "bait and switch." The consumer thinks they are the proud participants of democracy, but when the smoke clears, there are many strings attached that few have noticed that our elected officials are not the least interested in looking out for the interest, safety, and well-being of we the American people.

You and I are told we are participants in the new global economy, and very little can be done by our hardworking, dedicated, confounded, apologetic congressional representatives to change the status quo. This is the biggest line of BS ever perpetrated on we the people that I have ever heard.

Do we Americans know what we are nodding our heads in agreement to?

The big business bosses and bureaucrats merely use democratic principles as window dressing to initiate agreement or compliance they may need to accomplish the objectives of self-enrichment, power and control.

The American People Have Said—What?

The possibility to live the American dream has not been erased altogether, but it has been smeared to a haze for those who depend on someone else to make a place where it is possible.

There is an old saying, "Pull yourself up by your bootstraps." In order for a person to pull themselves up by their bootstraps, they most likely excel in being highly motivated and sufficiently educated, and possess strong entrepreneurial ambitiousness. There are many people who are able to pull themselves up by their bootstraps. There are a lot more people who do not have the qualities to reach their highest potential totally on their own.

"I only made a place where others can do it." I have borrowed this wisdom from a gentleman who spoke to an audience of his employees. He was a highly esteemed company executive, with a stellar leadership record. He was asked what he attributed to his time-honored success.

He said, "I only made a place where others could do it."

Government Should Not Do for Us What We Should Do for Ourselves

The same is true with our governmental leaders. In a general sense, it is the obligation of their office to make a place where their constituents are enabled or empowered with the possibility to achieve their highest potential.

Washington has a history of making a place where the corporations can do it. They have used the power of their office to clear obstacles in the free flow of commerce. If laws or a change in policy was needed, they served as legalists and policy changers on behalf of investors.

As the best example to support this, take a look at Bill Clinton granting China "most favored nation" status (MFNS) in 1994. Shortly thereafter, over two million American jobs went to China. On January 1, 1995, the WTO was established. Who do you suppose benefited from that (betterment for mankind) organization? By year 2000, the loss of American jobs was in free fall. So much for the workings of the WTO, IMF, UN, etc.

Washington bureaucrats certainly have not ignored capitalists to make a way for them; neither should they ignore the masses of Americans who have seen their jobs disappear to economies operating on a much-lower scale than that of America.

It is time for our elected to make a place where others can do it. They should initiate a new direction that fosters possibility versus impossibility, prosperity versus poverty, and confidence versus fear. Just what do they need to do to make that possible, you may ask? They need to admit to all the wrongdoing that has been done for the past forty years in economic policy and trade deals that gut America's economy and keep struggling foreign economies to remain stagnant.

The time has come for American leaders to think about what is good for the American worker equally to corporate profiteering. This kind of ethical, moral, and social leadership direction will make a place where others can reach their highest economic potential—in other words, live the American dream.

America was not founded with a society of the best and the brightest, and to believe that we will eventually be populated with only the best and brightest, as the only way to solve society's problems, is to deceive ourselves.

Let me be direct. If everyone were a physics professor or the equivalent, we could not function very long as a society. There is a reason why everyone is born with individual personalities and certain qualities, characteristics and abilities that makes each of us unique. Ordinary people who accomplished extraordinary things is what has made America great.

Let's mention a few Americans who contributed greatly to our outstanding economy.

Such was George Eastman, founder of Kodak Corp. Eastman was a high school dropout.

Bill Gates, founder of Microsoft Corp., was a college dropout.

Andrew Carnegie, his story is one of the most famous rags-to-riches accounts in United States history.

Not everyone wants to become an Eastman, Gates, or Carnegie, but most everyone does want to work in an environment that pays enough for them to be able to afford a decent home, food, and clothing.

Now, leading policymakers can't promise the people that by creating the environment that destroys our homeland economy by promoting the outsourcing of jobs and national treasure. That kind of leadership is not management at all. It does nothing to protect our citizens nor ensure national security.

I can tell you what this kind of leadership does, though: It creates an environment that amounts to resettlement of whole segments of a society. I recall Lew Dobbs, a famous TV and radio commentator, often commenting, "Don't the American people deserve a government that works?"

The diversity of America is what made her great once, and I suspect that our ability to respect diversity will play an important role in making her great again.

Is It True, the More Things Change, the More They Remain the Same?

The effectiveness of organized labor has come full circle. Industrial workers started with nothing, and it appears almost certain that big businesses have a master plan to take the position of unions back to the starting line.

If we were to view the last half of the twentieth century to that of a growing season, it would look and sound similar to this: We plowed the ground, sowed the seed, nurtured, watered, weeded, and finally harvested. And then the season was over, the plants died, and the ground lays fallow, waiting patiently and with enthusiasm for a new sower of seed to come once again.

This analogy depicts the rise and fall of the working people over the last century. We are waiting for someone to come along and make a way for us to start the American dream anew once again!

We have only taken a small sampling of how companies such as United Technologies has enlarged their footprint. Carrier Corp. amounts to little more than a flash in the pan to them. United Tech is worldwide in industrial manufacturing, aerospace and defense, construction, electronics, security products, and services.

Does the company cultivate ties with Congress? If so, how? Companies dependent on government contracts frequently lobby for spending on particular defense programs.

Any company you can think of will almost invariably reveal similar holdings, operate from so many different points, and access Congress in like manner. The point is that when a corporation becomes so big, owning or having invested interest in such vast holdings, it is said, "they cannot be allowed to go bankrupt because of the negative impact it would have on the whole country."

Something is wrong with this picture. Exactly how were they even able to accumulate such monumental wealth while whining about corporate taxes? If Congress lowers their tax rate, will they empty those offshore bank accounts and resettle in the USA, or will they do something else?

Many of them are so intertwined as global that they will never meet the definition as American again, but that does not mean that they cannot contribute to America's economic well-being once again rather than just sucking the life blood from us by manufacturing on foreign soil and exporting to the USA. Our congressional leadership only needs to step up to the plate and do their job in righting our trade policies gone amok) by forty years of corporate coddling.

We are showing growth rates in both the number of billionaires and in the poor, while the middle class continues to shrink. That positively tells us that the wealthier have advantage for increasing their prosperity while those in the middle are losing so much economic ground that they are joining the working poor.

The middle class, to a large extent, existed because of opportunity created by corporate America doing business in the USA in the form of trickle-down economics. When trickle down no longer existed because corporate America moved on, it (in a nutshell) destabilized our entire economy.

This is the synopsis that in one line describes the rise and fall of the middle class in America. The middle class were indeed recipients of trickle-down economics.

Looking Down the Road of Long Term

The day would come when a threshold of how many hardworking middle class taxpayers who have disappeared would reveal that there is not enough cash cows left to pay America's bills. Example, if a dairy farmer was such an incompetent manager as to sell off his best milk producers, his income is going to shrink.

Politicians didn't seem to understand this simple principle when they sold out American interests in the form of free trade and nodded to the admirers of the new global economy. What did they think it would lead to?

In addition to the middle class keeping commerce afloat, all governmental agencies that collect tax monies are greatly dependent on the middle-class taxpayers to fund the public coffers to pay the police, teachers, fire departments, and any of the hundreds of tax-supported agencies that every community depends on to keep society's services funded and running. When this type of economy was gone, where did our resourceful political leaders go looking for funds?

All we need to do is take a close look at what has happened to the States creating gambling in the form of lotteries, etc. If you are thinking this is only pocket change, think again. The people who can afford gambling their financial resources least are spending 5, 10, 15, 20 dollars per week and some much more on lotteries trying to hit it rich.

When you apply what millions of the more poor people are giving up of their meager incomes that amounts to huge (tax) revenues. I am reluctant to believe that well to do folks are as diligent in investing in lottery tickets! Actually, what lotteries amount to is new and higher taxes levied (voluntarily) on the middle and working poor class.

Rather than getting rid of the victims in the gas furnaces under the cover of darkness, by shutting down the blast furnaces of the American industrial revolution, they effectively got rid of the high cost of labor. One by one, year after year, the working ranks were shrinking in both size and status.

Between do-nothing Congresses to involve themselves for the betterment of both domestic and foreign workers, the courts were no friend either of American workers in general, and union workers in particular were not making any steps forward but only two steps back.

Let me be absolutely clear. Not only was our US Congress no friend of American workers, but also the American court system rarely stood with workers in domestic labor-dispute issues. At the international level, the UN member nations and the WTO member nations have demonstrated hostility to the International Labor Organization (ILO) foreign workers' rights, and literally excluded worker representatives from meetings at the UN and WTO. The very global agencies that everyone thinks are looking out for humanity at large are the very agencies that are looking out for and giving favorable advantage to the corporations.

As I found out how one-sided the meetings, the dialogue, the intent, and the goals of the UN, the WTO, and the IMF (International Monetary Fund) were, I see that it is clearly concerning that the global economy looks more like a high-level conspiracy for absolute control over financing, production, low-cost labor, and disregard for human rights, and distribution of goods and services around the globe.

In the United States—Beginning in the 1960s

For a time, factory workers followed the jobs until there was no place left to transfer to or to relocate and start anew. Ethnic cleansing could not have produced a more total annihilation than this form of economic extermination. Wholesale give backs in the form of contract concessions were widespread, under the guise of being competitive. The fact—after the fact was that, as Ross Perot would say, you cain't compete against emerging economies like that of Mexico at less than $2.50 per hour labor. It just cain't be done, folks!

What could or can be done, though, is to level the playing field. There has been little talk from time to time about leveling the playing field, as if politicians understood how to do it, but somehow it just never got off the drawing board. That is easy enough to understand.

Some economists actually viewed the transition for America from a manufacturing economy to a services economy as a step forward and a better direction for the sophisticated society they were becoming. After all, *they* were investing in foreign opportunity alongside the corporations that were building corporate wealth.

It may be an arguable issue if our Washington bureaucrats merely nodded in agreeing to outsource American manufacturing without penalties to re-import and, at the same time, failure to develop a comprehensive master plan is the critical piece missing to qualify as good stewardship of American interests and protecting we the people.

Protecting the American people is job number 1 of the White House and Congresses, and that is not against foreign and domestic enemies in a military sense only, but against all threats that endanger the life and liberty of we the people—period!

Had a master plan (among nations) mandating a comprehensive commitment to the affected nations been on the table, the transfer of assets and jobs would invariably been managed, addressing transition equality within affected nations, developing true prosperity in underdeveloped regions would have gone a long way toward avoiding economic anarchy.

We must be reminded that corporations create business plans for the advancing fifty years. It appears as though

Washington never had a plan to manage international commerce from one week to the next, and even when the ensuing crisis of monumental trade deficit between the USA and China evolved, there was not even a crisis reaction from our leadership.

What does this reaction tell us? It tells us with all assurances that the multinationals are in complete control and our political establishment is only along for the ride.

State lotteries—Business plan or tax plan?

State and national lotteries may have been a crafty and creative move to make up lost coffer monies, but they represent a disgraceful alternative to justify annihilating the middle class.

While the trade war with China is associated with the 1990s onward, it must be understood that by transferring jobs by the millions to China, de-capitalizing the American workforce began about twenty years earlier (1970s). As we have discussed, the economically weakened position of the USA did not happen overnight.

De-capitalizing working Americans seems to be the most accurate explanation as to why our roads and bridges are in disrepair. We have dropped so low in funding that the thought of developing a modernized infrastructure to allow the USA a world-class economic leader status is more of a hopeless dream than an actual reality.

The USA as a superpower status is on the edge of a cliff. Much if not most of a generation of middle class has been exterminated, and Washington's best response is to play the free-trade card. Sighting, honoring free-trade policies as an economic cost does not absolve them of their responsibilities to craft fair (not free) trade in the global arena.

Suggesting that displaced workers "go back to school" was suggested in the late 90s onward, and some retraining and assistance programs were made available for displaced workers. This sounded like a great suggestion, and right, under the desperate crisis circumstances. However, a Band-Aid is no treatment nor a cure for a cancerous condition.

Retraining or furthering one's education is always a healthy approach for a worker's progressive financial security, but this government program was seemingly targeted toward workers who were forced out of work rather than taking a chosen pathway. It would only work for a handful, who had been in the workforce less than ten years, but for those who have been working fifteen and twenty years, starting over again would not be easy.

In actuality, it looked more like a resettlement program for war-torn refugees. Retraining amounted more to another means of temporary unemployment income for a job market that did not exist.

China Given Most Favored Trade Partner Status—Bill Clinton (1994)

To say that a strong manufacturing base is essential to our national security is a seriously bold and risky statement for any politician in lite of their job description. One such was Mike Huckabee, Republican presidential candidate 2008. Huckabee said it, and not one other Republican or Democrat has ever disagreed with that ideal.

Doesn't it make you wonder why our Democratic leadership was eager and worked hard to give China the political tools, namely "most valued nation" status under Bill Clinton and China's induction into the WTO? Once in the WTO, China began mounting a monumental US trade imbalance. Not only that, Washington sees no problem whatsoever in continuing this economic course.

It is worthy of mention that we commonly refer to China as a competitor nation that rose up all by themselves to confront the USA in the global economic arena. This writer does not believe that is the total truth. As Paul Harvey, the renowned commentator would say, "Here is the rest of the story."

Following WWII, the USA rebuilt Japan with American investment, technology, etc. As it has been said about the wisdom of a good father concerning his up and coming son,

"I taught him all I knew, he should have learned something on his own."

And so it was with Japan. Indeed they did learn something on their own! In the course of thirty years, Japan rose up to knock the economic socks off the USA.

Initially, American companies either moved production operations to Japan or invested in business operations, thereby handing over intellectual properties. Sounds familiar? Once the opportunities ran their course in Japan, another opportunity opened up: China. The main difference is that corporate America also learned something on their own.

However, the White House and our sitting Congresses never caught on to what was happening right under their noses. Or maybe it was too lucrative for their personal war chest, as they call it, to give a damn about the plight of American jobs and our national security.

Yes, indeed, American manufacturing went a long way in providing China with jobs, investment, intellectual properties, etc. If USA could be sighted as a bear for punishment, the China situation, coupled with the insertion of giving broad powers to the World Trade Organization (WTO), has knocked our economic socks off, not to mention put our national security in a headlock.

As Lew Dobbs, national commentator, has so appropriately expressed, "Can't we have government that works?"

Again, the classic behavior of the WTO is to grant favor to developing nations. Why is that, you may say? Well, let's consider the advantages for the multinationals once again: cheap labor, lax environmental regulations, profitability, and the WTO has replaced GATT.

GATT: a United Nations agency created by a multinational treaty to promote trade by the reduction of tariffs and import quotas General Agreement on Tariffs and Trade.

Definition:

1. General Agreement on Tariffs and Trade, an international treaty (1948–94) to promote trade and economic development by reducing tariffs and other restrictions. It was superseded by the establishment of the World Trade Organization in 1995.

Have you noticed by now? GATT, WTO, the UN or others—they are all agencies and usually, if not exclusively, a part of the United Nations; in other words, a part of the new world order or the new global economy, used interchangeably.

The common theme in conspiracy theories about a New World Order is that a secretive power elite with a globalist agenda is conspiring to eventually rule the world through an authoritarian world government, which will replace sovereign nation-states, and an all-encompassing propaganda whose ideology hails the establishment of the New World Order as the culmination of history's progress.

Simply put, the promised benefits of trade liberalization with China have been unfulfilled.

Trade liberalization has not gone unfulfilled for the corporations. It has accomplished exactly what they were planning in the way of profits, profits, profits.

At this writing, the USA would like to invest in reversing the effects of global warming by reducing our carbon footprint. To do this on equal footing with economically booming China represents many difficulties because of such rapid growth that has taken place in China. Not to mention uniformity, conformity, and standardization of products.

With startups sprouting almost overnight, it is difficult to track what is happening. For instance, lead in paint for toys and hazardous chemicals in sheet rock for buildings made in China have been identified. While the USA is compelled by environmental and product standards for pollution and safety, China observes no such rules; how can anyone compete against that? This is where global trade rules of engagement should have been implemented.

- Meet product standard, or there is no export.
- Meet environmental standard specifications, or there is no export.
- Meet worker health and safety standard rules, or there is no export.

Lest we forget, much of the export products we are talking about are not Chinese products but rather American companies that have relocated production in China. To say American manufactured goods cannot compete against Chinese in this scenario is only half-true at best. It is American companies exporting American products using Chinese-labor-made products back to the USA. The truth is the corporations are only comparing one labor force against another for their product.

While all this is coming from China, we must keep in mind that US companies carrying on production are ramping up monumental profits by conforming to China's slack regulations and enjoying cheap Chinese labor rates. It's all being done with the WTO exerting their given powers to supersede national sovereignty and favor developing nations.

Why would the WTO favor developing nations? Maybe it's at the urging of the multinationals looking for profitable opportunities. When you look at almost any American brand or company that once existed and was produced and marketed from American soil, and now those same products carry the label "Made in China," that about explains it all about who is competing against who.

Was middle-class America left out and left behind? With all things considered, is it unreasonable to take the negative view that the American economy and American workers' plight looked more like a resettlement program for war-torn refugees?

Workers in Impoverished Nations Don't Know the Difference

Poverty is the shame richer nations should deplore, as well as poorer nations should come to the defense of their impoverished workers in sweatshops. The human hope is that eventually the workers will be better off. Eventually being better off is far from the level of expectations of investors, so is it reasonable or fair to make workers struggle and wait twenty or thirty years to elevate their standard of living, while corporations are working overtime to find places to reinvest immediate profits?

Example, when Carrier Corp. shut down in Lewisburg, Tennessee, and Syracuse, New York, and moved manufacturing to China, first-year operating profit rose 54 percent. That was easy!

The following is what the aims of the United Nations Charter says member nations are committed to: to achieve international cooperation in solving economic, social, cultural, and humanitarian problems and in promoting respect for human rights and fundamental freedoms.

If we are not careful or diligent, we will find ourselves being dictated to by an entity called the new world order, and we will be compelled to bow to the tenets of such agencies as the World Trade Organization to decide our international trade policies and the United Nations council to decide our international human relations and intervention policies.

The United Nations has the paperwork to prove that they talk the talk, but walking the walk is not a match. The World Trade Organization made no bones to de-invite the International Labor Organization to attend an important meeting to discuss international worker rights, says a lot toward the rest of the story.

The workings of the UN, WTO, ILO, and IMF appear to interact with nations at the governing level, but ultimately, their resolutions and policies greatly affect workers more than operational edicts. All with the exception of the International Monetary Fund, which has the ability to dictate requirements to usually poor nations with loans that give the IMF great power, and are able to insist that governments adopt certain policies as a condition for receiving funds.

In a Global Economy, We Need to Define What World-Class Means

Investorwords.com's definition of *economy*: "Activities related to the production and distribution of goods and services in a particular geographic region. The correct and effective use of available resources."

They certainly can talk the talk, but there is no one willing to hold their feet to the fire. The question of the hour is, where is the greatest superpower on planet Earth in all this?

Our Congresses purport to hold dear and near high ethical, moral, and social standards when they invoke their service to the American people. Accordingly, not only am I surprised but also I am aghast that they seem to be wearing ear-protective devices when it comes to observing even some of the mission statements and ethics published as guiding principles of domestic and global economic and peace-keeping agencies.

Don't get the wrong idea that I am talking about dictating against free enterprise in someone else's country, but without standardized rules, there is no game. There is no fair playing field. Plenty, and all the safeguards to protect the American economy and the American worker is available and lies within reach of our legislators; it is just a case of getting them to do their job.

Now, on the other hand, even they will have to go up against the world goons, namely the World Trade Organization, the UN, and all the others that give the false impression that they are advocates of workers' rights. You and I must ask, who are the member nations of the WTO, UN, IMF, etc., that we are talking about? Who are the staff members? Where do they draw the voting representatives from, etc.?

I don't believe I would be too far from accurate to believe people from the corporate, financial, and political circles make up the roster. With that in mind, is it any wonder that ILO representatives were denied attending meetings in the WTO?

At the urging—or is it insistence?—of the multinational corporations, they have empowered the World Trade Organization to do that piece of dirty work for them. Remember, any nation who joins the WTO signs away their sovereign rights of domestic law and agree to abide by WTO rules. And just who does the WTO work for? My guess is that it is the multinationals, based on who seem to always come out on the top end.

What have I been saying about calling such actions perpetrated on not just Americans but also on all working people of the world? This is political and economic control! It may be legal, it may be nonviolent, and it may be silent, but it looks like control, it smells like control, and it is producing much of the same results that terrorism produces in social, economic, social, and moral values. We can call it what it really is, or we can bury our head in the sand and pretend that it is something else.

There is a distinctive difference between global anarchy and global collaboration, responsibility, and ethical management for a level playing field between trading nations. That means looking out for the emerging and the older trading partners alike.

To think that something as big as the global economy can function freely is the poorest determination and an irresponsible action of ethics imaginable. If you are thinking that is precisely what the WTO's function is, you would be right. That is what they are *supposed* to do. However, they are so openly working for the multinational corporations that their humanitarian function is a complete joke. By now, it should be pretty well understood that if our own government fails to look out for the interests of the American people, no one else will.

All systems of financing, production, distribution, and consumption are interconnected and relative, or the financial collapse of 2008 would not have been global.

http://www.america.gov/st/washfile-english/2005/August/20050824162913adynned4.766482e-02.html

The United Nations' aims, according to the fact sheet, are set out in the preamble to the UN Charter: "To maintain international peace and security; to develop friendly relations among nations; to achieve international cooperation in solving (economic), social, cultural, and humanitarian problems and in promoting (respect for human rights) and fundamental freedoms; and to be a center for harmonizing the actions of nations in attaining these common ends."

We the people should ask the UN Council just how they define the terms *cooperation*, *promoting*, and *respect*. If they have no intentions of addressing economic problems, why do they even bother to put it in writing? Just what does the United Nations Council mean or intend when they say "promoting respect for human rights"?

The above is just one paragraph concerning the broad scope for a working agenda of the United Nations. While I tend to think of the UN as mostly a peace-keeping force in the world arena, I would be prone to let them off the hook for having a low profile in dealing with world economic issues.

That being said, if you notice though, they also keep a low profile in peace-keeping issues. It is my opinion that they are about one of the most useless organizations in existence. The good ole USA seems to always be the predominate player and often sole contributor in world-peace efforts.

At the global level, it is all talk and little, if any, action that supports workers' interests, human rights, and dignity or anything that is relative just simply is not only ignored but also erased from their agenda altogether. When they say, "To be a center for harmonizing the actions of nations in attaining these common ends," somebody, please clear out the smoke.

There are currently 192 member states that belong to the UN.

Based on their erroneous inconsistent actions and lack of meaningful accomplishments, it is questionable if the UN is a help or a hindrance to international peace and security.

The Record of the UN

After the Holocaust, the world said, "Never again." Never again will we stand by and watch while millions are slaughtered.

After the Cambodian genocide of the 1970s, the world said, "Never again."

After the Rwandan genocide of 1994, the world said, "Never again."

After the mass killings in Srebenica (in Bosnia) in 1995, the world said, "Never again."

Probably in 2008 the world will say, "Never again," after the slow-motion genocide in Sudan is finally brought to its terrible completion. The UN does not have a very impressive record of accomplishment in any of the areas they claim to be an advocate.

Following the 9-11-2001 attack on the World Trade Center, it took the world's superpower a mere six weeks to draw up the tenants and pass the controversial Patriot Act.

How big is too big

There without doubt are many reasons why a company may want to shut down a manufacturing facility in America and move that operation to a foreign nation, but their salivation for cheap labor should not be one of them.

An example of what I mean is this: when Carrier Corporation closed manufacturing plants in Lewisburg, Tennessee, in March 2002 and Syracuse, New York, in October 2003, it was, to quote, "to shift the production to plants in China and Singapore."

WWW.ANSWERS.COM/TOPIC/CARRIER-CORPORATION: Ending sixty-six years of Carrier manufacturing in the Syracuse area. The company planned to leave behind a reduced workforce of 1,600 people employed in marketing, sales, product support, warehousing, engineering, and research.

Carrier has several other US-based plants, and some of the affected employees were given transfers, but most were not. Folks, we are talking about some 2,300 US jobs between just these two plant closings. These are faceless individuals to corporate officials, but to the middle class, these are workers left high and dry.

Between 2001 and 2003, these and other bottom-line-oriented initiatives yielded results: operating profits jumped 54 percent, from $590 million to $911 million.

During the same period, revenues were relatively stagnant, increasing only 4 percent, from $8.9 billion to $9.25 billion. Just another case of global trade made easier.

That move was wonderful for Carrier (United Technologies) even though it represents an indirect chipping away at our national security. Why should our American Congress be concerned? No one is going to notice that one of their responsibilities is to "regulate commerce with foreign nations."

I am sure they do some regulating, but not in any meaningful way that will inconvenience the industries, but rest assured, not only have American workers been inconvenienced but also their lives have been affected, like those we see of foreign civil war refugees migrating to resettle and start over.

If you think that capitalism is only an ultra-conservative notion, you would certainly be amiss. This idea of a new global economy belonged to the Liberal camp as well. As I have mentioned, when NAFTA was signed, every past, present, and still-living president was present and in full agreement to this trade agreement. Let me say that again: every past, present, and still-living president was present and in full agreement to the NAFTA trade agreement. It sure looks like corporate America sold this diversified group one hell of a bill of goods folks.

China represents a fast-growing market for Carrier's products, and rightly so, that Carrier would want a piece of the Chinese action. That which is manufactured in China should be consumed in China. Why? Because the USA has developed a higher standard of living and simply cannot compete with Chinese labor rates.

The Chinese market for Carrier air-conditioning units is growing. We applaud them for the venture to meet the market with Chinese manufactured products at Chinese labor rates. If Carrier insists on exporting some of their excess products back to the USA, the US Congress has the duty to "regulate commerce with foreign nations."

What should they do? What can they do? The obvious answer is to impose a tariff to level the playing field. There is a simple reason this has not been done. It's called lobbying. Congress thinks the American people are stupid and they demean us by their actions.

You may be wondering what else, if anything, can Congress do to level the playing field? Can our Congress require a company to pay foreign workers a higher wage? I believe the answer is yes, they can. They could be given options.

One option could be tariff, another could be some form of standardized worker wages. It is done all the time with companies doing work for federal and state projects in the USA. To get public-works projects, the bidding companies are required to pay workers a union scale wage. Can this policy be implemented in the global arena? After all, we have more than enough agencies that advocate worker concerns, namely the WTO, UN, ILO, just to name a few.

When an American company is in partnership with a foreign manufacturer, if agreement on wages is not feasible or possible, then an appropriate tariff certainly is and will quickly determine if trade between the USA and the country in question is feasible. Or depending on a nation-to-nation trade agreement it could and likely would help a corporation decide who and where their customer base exists, because they would either be confronted with import tariffs as well as coughed up a negotiated wage-adjustment scale in the host country. It would go a long way toward assuring corporate America that the day of a free lunch is over.

Remember, first-year profit for Carrier's move to China netted a 54 percent profit gain. What has United Technologies or Carrier been doing with profits? Here is a short list of a long history in reinvesting and subsidiary building. Do you suppose much of this is tax deductible?

- Carrier Air Conditioning Pty. Limited (Australia)
- Carrier Aircon Limited (India)
- Carrier China Limited (Hong Kong)
- Carrier Commercial Refrigeration, Inc.; Carrier Espana, SL (Spain)
- Carrier HVACR Investments B.V. (Netherlands)

- Carrier LG Limited (South Korea); Carrier Ltd. (South Korea)
- Carrier Mexico SA. de CV
- Carrier Nederland BV (Netherlands)
- Carrier Sales and Distribution, LLC; Carrier SAS (France)
- Carrier SpA (Italy)
- Carrier Singapore (PTE) Limited
- Carrier Transicold Europe SAS (France)
- International Comfort Products
- LLC; Misr Refrigeration and Air Conditioning Manufacturing Company SAE (Egypt)

The Foregoing (Taken from www.answers. com/topic/carrier-corporation)

I don't think any American would have a problem with Carrier having facilities in all these countries, as long as they are expanding their customer base in those countries. However, if they are also motivated to export back to the USA, there should be consequences that discourage this practice. Namely, those consequences are along the lines of what I have previously laid out. Those consequences would go a long way in protecting the American worker and preserving national security.

What did this move do for American society? We can assume that each air conditioner unit shipped back to the USA carried the same price sticker that it did when it was purchased (made in the USA), minus the payroll to American workers and minus the worker payroll tax revenues going into US coffers.

While the word *competition* remains a relative terminology, its significance bares little meaning as multinationals have such vast holdings that they often are only competing against themselves, making the word *competition* meaningless to them. The word *competition* is probably the world's most subverted word in the global economic environment.

You may be thinking how good it is for the corporate world to be making all these profits as it influences the stock market, and maybe your holdings if you are invested. We know how volatile the stock market is, and when adjustment happens, middle-class America often takes the brunt of loss that Wall Street professionals and big investors are insulated from.

If the volatility of the market were to be more stable between nations globally, would investors be able to participate with much less volatility and adjustments from time to time that can wipe out many 401s and IRAs?

Do the American people deserve better than a reactionary form of leadership?

Re-ac-tion-a-ry: extreme conservatism or rightism in politics, opposing political or social change.

On the corporate scene: Our politicians don't seem to understand or care that they are selling out to the corporate bosses who, quite frankly, my dear, don't give a damn about whether or not the USA is a superpower, and they most certainly could care less about those who wrestle with economic decline.

On the political scene: When the American people get to the point of clamoring for change or balancing the budget, what is the first thing politicians threaten we the people with? Of course, entitlement cuts, Social Security, Medicare, and Medicaid. That will shut us up, huh. Did you ever see anyone use such expertise in dodging the root of the problem and blaming someone else for what they themselves are primarily responsible for?

Until competent leadership begins to talk the talk and walk the walk and promote what constitutes an economy, becomes believed in and supported, we the people will be run over by those looking for opportunity.

Opportunity: The beginning of the end of the American industrial revolution had its silent but swift moving start. Remember, the USA began rebuilding Japan with the ending of World War II. American corporations saw the opportunity in cheap Japanese labor, they invested, and the idea caught on quickly, after which one and then another cheap labor source was added until the new global economy became the catchphrase.

The only thing that differentiates Japan from what is happening with China and Mexico is magnitude. The rebuilding of Japan was one thing, but the creation of the WTO and Bill Clinton granting China most-favored-nation status (MFN) was a direct hit that sunk the ship. NAFTA was so misrepresented as good fortune for all players that the promoters should be ashamed and embarrassed.

Maquilar or Opportunity?

Why is it called the maquiladora or maquila industry? Private investment and government involvement from both the USA and Mexico initiated a study conducted by the Arthur D. Little Foundation that took place in Ciudad Juarez in 1965.

A US researcher Dick Bowlin and a Mexico-based analyst conducted a study to alleviate the growing Mexican unemployment rate along the Northern Mexican border regions. The maquila program was initially known as the "Border Industrialization Program." However, over time, two key buzzwords, *maquiladora* and *twin plant*, were coined by the researchers.

The researchers chose "maquiladora" or "maquila" because it is derived from the old Spanish word *maquilar*, which means "to mill." Historically, a wheat farmer would hire a miller to grind his crop. The farmer would then compensate the miller with a portion of the grain. Such a relationship indicated a production-sharing process between the producer and the manufacturer, and as such, *maquilar* was applied to the industry.

The second buzzword was *twin plant*, which was coined by Bowlin to emphasize the joint effort between two operations: one in Mexico and one in the USA. Joint effort is an understatement!

Who owns these maquiladoras?

At the moment, there are twenty-seven countries participating in the maquiladora or twin plant program, with the majority of foreign ownership by US companies. The USA is the only country that has exported a lion's share of wealth and jobs to Mexico. The USA represents the wheat farmer who is hiring a miller in Mexico to grind his crop into a high-value finished product. The only difference is that USA corporate money owns the grist mill in Mexico, and they are doing a good job at making sure Mexican workers remain accustomed to a standard of living that they have become accustomed to.

How many plants are there, and where are they located?

As of December 2002, there were 3,285 registered maquiladoras in Mexico, employing 1.1 million Mexican workers. However, 69 percent of these plants are located within one to thirty miles from the US–Mexico border, of which 1,683 are American owned.

The location of these plants speaks volumes about their intended purpose, but the clincher is that they are just over the border in one of the cheapest labor pools available. So much for the promise of thousands of high-paying jobs under NAFTA.

The Foregoing from www.Solunet-Infomex.Com

Concerning Mexico, after you decipher some of the statistical values, are you still wondering why illegal immigration is rampant? Wonder no more! The average unskilled factory worker in one of these maquiladoras is $4.85 per day. That is per day!

I could not believe this statistic, so I did more research and found testimonies that are all over the page, so to speak, but judging from what we see in our immigration problem, we have to conclude that Mexico is, in many ways, like the USA. We have the ultra rich, and we have the working poor, only with a larger gap. Have no fear, the gap is widening in the USA all the time.

Mexican Testimonials

I have family in Monterrey. My brother-in-law earns approximately $60 USD per week. He is a supervisor in a garage for buses. This is a pretty good job. He works six days a week, about nine hours a day. Of course, there is no such thing as overtime.

My other brother-in-law works in a factory in Monterrey that makes spandex clothing (exercise stuff) and makes about $45 per week working a different shift every month. Also a decent job.

My *suegra* lives in Cd. Mante and cleans house for a pretty well-off family for about $30 per week.

The Juarez Disaster

The principal reason for moving businesses to Mexico is because of ridiculously cheap labor costs, which was the main goal of the maquiladoras. A functionalist would say that the maquiladoras were intended to bring people jobs and provide lower costs. The low cost of living and the low cost of labor in Juarez is the manifest function of the whole maquiladoras system.

Juarez was mainly a tourist town; they based most of their income on tourists coming to the city. The maquiladoras was aimed at bringing jobs and income to the city and bringing hope to the people who didn't have much to look forward to. This was a good system to start up because it helped the city develop into a large industrialized city, yet it was bad because it brought along latent functions such have higher crime rates, and murders.

A functionalist would probably blame the murders of the women on the industry. Not only did the maquiladoras bring along jobs and pay, but also so many people would come and go and be hired and fired that it also brought some poverty as well. The jobs that the system provided were not very high paying. The jobs paid only $2.00 an hour, and if the person was skilled or had any special talents that helped on the job, they may get a pay raise up to $2.50 an hour. This may not seem like much according to American standards, but for a community with such high poverty levels and low cost of living, this was just enough to get you by.

The above is public knowledge. If there is reason to disbelieve the accuracy of this student term paper I have been unable to find other information as specific as this. And it fits perfectly as a piece in the puzzle. It also holds the capitalists' feet to the fire about the promises of NAFTA to create thousands of high-paying jobs. But wouldn't you suspect that they would say $2.00 per hour is high pay in Mexico, and with a straight face to boot?

Let's be reminded again, it is in the job description of Congress to manage international trade, not the job of corporations. It is obvious that for the last forty years Congress has done only one thing in this respect: they have acted in the interests of the corporations and thrown the American workers under the bus and passed it off as the new global economy, as if it was totally out of their control.

Not only that, but they have put blame on the nations for such economic woes rather than on their cozy relationship with the corporations. All you have to do to make sense of this is to ask yourself who are the political campaign contributors?

Not only every sitting Congress but also right up to White House leadership under George W. Bush, who in his last days in the White House attempted to add the Transatlantic Trade and Investment (TTIP) agreement to his legacy.

Again, under Obama's administration, his aim was to go down in history as the one who achieved the TTIP agreement. Why was getting this all-time biggest trade deal passed so important? For both Bush and Obama, it was a matter of personal achievement only. Of course it had nothing to do for the betterment of American workers or our country's best interest. It was all about putting more power into the hands of pharmaceuticals, investors, banking, food, manufacturing, and every other industry that our lives depend on.

Not only that but also it empowered the corporations to dictate or sue if necessary nations that imposed warning labels on certain products, such as tobacco etc. Germany's chancellor Merkel described TTIP as a "win-win situation" that "could set global standards" by creating a free-trade area unlike any before it.

Do you recall me using the term "corporate communism"? Well, the above is one of the best examples of what I'm talkin' about. Too much power in the wrong hands. In this instance, I will have to say we the people have had a win in stalling TTIP as it stands.

As I have stated, and I will say it again, where the rubber meets the road, there is only ten cents worth of difference between modern-day Democratic and Republican parties.

What Could Be Contributing to Poverty and Immigration Problems for Mexicans?

After almost twenty generations of intermarriage between whites and Indians, Mexico has ended up with an almost-wholly white elite, a vast mixed-race (mestizo) working class, and at least ten million extremely impoverished pure Indians who have never assimilated into Hispanic culture. And the ruling class is becoming ever whiter.

Power to the Plutocrats

The power that such men and a select few others wield in Mexico can hardly be exaggerated. The popular press commonly writes of the three hundred ruling families of Mexico, or of the seventy men who run the economy. The conglomerates' grip on the economy is indeed formidable.

Mexico's Corrupt Elite Pays Itself Well

Writing for the Center for Immigration Studies (CIS), George W. Grayson, a professor of government at the College of William and Mary, reports on how well the corrupt Mexican elite pays itself while they demand that the American people pay for the backwardness of Mexico.

- President Vicente Fox ($236,693) makes more than the leaders of France ($95,658), the UK ($211,434), and Canada ($75,582).

- Although they are in session only a few months a year, Mexican deputies take home at least $148,000—substantially more than their counterparts in France ($78,000), Germany ($105,000), and congressmen throughout Latin America.

- At the end of the three-year term, Mexican deputies voted themselves a $28,000 "leaving-office bonus."

- Members of the thirty-two state legislatures ($60,632) earn on average twice the amount earned by US state legislators ($28,261). The salaries and bonuses of the lawmakers in Baja,

California ($158,149), Guerrero ($129,630), and Guanajuato ($111,358) exceed the salaries of legislators in California ($110,880), the District of Columbia ($92,500), Michigan ($79,650), and New York ($79,500).

- Members of the city council of Saltillo, San Luis Potosí, not only received a salary of $52,778 in 2005, but also awarded themselves a $20,556 end-of-year bonus.

- Average salaries (plus Christmas stipends known as *aguinaldos*) place the average compensation of Mexican state executives at $125,759, which exceeds by almost $10,000 the mean earnings of their US counterparts ($115,778). On average, governors received *aguinaldos* of $14,346 in 2005—a year when 60 percent of Mexicans received no year-end bonuses.

It is noteworthy that the Bush clan has many friends in Mexico's corrupt elite. George W. Bush looks at Mexico's elite and sees kindred spirits.

Returning to the Center for Immigration Studies (CIS) report, Mexico's elite pays itself handsomely while investing little in the education of its people and expecting the American people to pay for the failures of Mexico.

I have constantly referred to Mexico as the classic example where manufacturers are attracted to relocate because of such low-cost opportunities. This business model is duplicated over and over no matter where they go. By citing Mexico, can you even imagine what the opportunities corporate America has been able to tap into in China and other places?

I will grant you that this business model appears conflicting about the creation of poverty from the standpoint that emerging economies, where the wealth and jobs have been transferred benefit quite well according to collective economic reports and headlining data. But the reality is that the benefits to impoverished nations are marginal and moving from extreme poverty to moderate poverty, and by the time the position of workers in these emerging economies finally reach an economic status that could be classifies as prosperous, the capitalists investors will be moving on to their next targeted feeding ground.

The process has once again cycled out. The rich will retain more of the world's wealth, and the poor will be kept in check. You would think that the spread of the world's wealth would become more evenly divided among the world's population as time goes on because of capitalistic investors cycling through or reaching saturation as emerging economies mature.

For instance, we have seen capitalism cycle when Japan became the primary emerging economy after World War II. It took Japan or Taiwan about forty years to lose the interests of investors. When, Japan's standard of living began to look much like that of the USA. Investors began looking for better feeding grounds in terms of low-cost labor, lax environmental, and corporate regulation laws.

We, the American people, have heard the term "global economy" so often and for so long we have become desensitized as to what the term really means. It's like the word *reform*; in most instances, people believe reform is for their betterment, when in fact, reform may mean just the opposite.

Global Economy Is Like No Other

Mismatched economies simply cannot be thrown in the arena as equal competitors.

Working people around the world are interested in equality, possibly more than anything else, and they are not actively experiencing it simply because big business is more interested in control and maintaining the status quo. Global has more to do with domination and New World Order than economic benefit for all.

I personally believe that Barack Obama was elected in a landslide victory in 2008 simply because Americans believed that he had the ability as he said, "We (must) bring back the middle class." The American people will wait, watch, and evaluate, and there will be an election again in four years.

When We Tell It the Way It Really Is

Ross Perot financed his own campaign and was indebted to no one. He garnered 19 percent of the 1992 popular vote, which was a historic fete for an independent.

Ross Perot was not one to mince words. He is remembered by many Americans for his down-home folksy description of the "sucking" sound you would hear as US jobs leave for Mexico under the NAFTA trade agreement.

Note: NAFTA was signed just months after the 1992 presidential run by President Bill Clinton.

Again, in 1996, Perot supporters were excitedly anticipating him to run again, but the dirty tactics of his would-be opponents and the biased treatment by the media caused him to reconsider whether he would run. Although he had not yet announced his candidacy, the news media accused him of abruptly withdrawing from the race after getting supporters' hopes up.

As a history buff trying to analyze why Perot abruptly chose not to run, I believe he considered the depth of sleaze that was perpetrated toward a family member and came to the conclusion that was only the first example of incompetent unprofessional dirty tactics that he would have to battle in the White House. He chose his family.

Much debate has been had since Ross Perot vied for the presidency. It was closer than any Independent candidate has ever come to winning the Oval Office, and many believe that had he run the second time around he would have won.

It is my personal belief that Deep State politics is so embedded in both the Democratic and Republican parties to the extent that main line constituents were not ready for the kind of change that an independent (maverick), like Perot, was prepared to lead our nation in unchartered waters.

A Different Time, a Different Place

In today's economy, many people are putting party aside and looking for a leader who has demonstrated competence and character with corresponding evidence of proven effectiveness and integrity. As a person, Ross Perot possessed those credentials. His supporters placed greater confidence in his ability based on his personal achievements and his record as a businessman than anyone to step up to the plate in modern times.

Perot will always be remembered for his charts. Not only did he bring his charts along, but also he took the time to explain the essence of what the charts tended to prove. Even today, when issues in and around the Belt Way get tough,

Washington legislators have been known to say, "Where is Ross Perot when you need him?"

Perot was a great believer in what we call the airlines philosophy). Airline passenger safety training preceding takeoff advises passengers in the event that the cabin loses air pressure and the oxygen masks deploy, adults administer oxygen to themselves first and then attend to their children.

While that sounds selfish, self-preserving, and anti-heroic we know that if you cannot function effectively, you will be ineffective in saving anyone around you either. Ross Perot believed this was sound judgment to focus on "fixing America's economy first" so that the USA could afford to become an effective world leader and peacemaker.

If Perot had been successful in gaining the presidency, would we be in the situation with China as a super economic power, and would we continue to have the situation with Mexico that we have? Perot's background for success made him for sure look like a man with a plan, and not one to merely react to each crisis as it rears its ugly head.

Anyone can make a mistake. It's what you do to make a correction that counts.

Although NAFTA was signed during Bill Clinton's administration, it was initially drafted during George H. Bush's administration and had the support of all the following presidents prior to Clinton's first term: President Clinton,

President Bush, President Carter, President Ford, and Vice President Gore. All endorsed the NAFTA trade agreement.

There is a full transcript of a meeting held in the East Room of the White House on September 14, 1993, with speeches by each of the former presidents mentioned and an opening introduction by then-vice president Al Gore. You can read exactly what each former president said supporting the document as a recorded transcript for press release at the following Internet address: www.historycentral.com/Documents/Clinton/SigningNaFTA.html.

They all supported NAFTA (Republican and Democratic administrations alike). Because they all supported NAFTA does not mean that they were poor leaders. But after fifteen years of being duped with false promises, you would think many things have been learned as to what was deficient with the agreement, and that a radical fresh overhaul of the agreement is needed to correct this malfeasance and for future trade agreements if we are to halt the de-capitalization of America, deepening world poverty and the further eradication of the homeland middle class.

Up until the day George W. Bush left office in 2008, he remained a staunch believer in pursuing even more free-trade deals seemingly with no safeguards for American jobs or national security. George W. Bush did the things that seem to paint him into a picture of favoring the elite at the expense of working people. Here is how I see it.

George W. Bush supported wholesale immigration for his corporate friends. He supported bailouts for the auto industry and banks at the same time demanding pay cuts to the auto workers. He was a proponent for more trade deals even with the advent of the NAFTA failure. There are reports of his close ties with the corrupt Mexican elite, and there is suspicion that the war with Iraq was an opportunity for the Halliburton Co. to make a bundle from that fiasco.

Only one year has elapsed since GM conceded the number one spot to Toyota (2007). Just one year since, it is now questionable if GM will even remain a viable US car company by year's end, 2008. Much of, if not most of, what has caused the failure of all three US car companies to decline is not in the ability of workers to compete.

Some would arguably say foreign automobiles are less expensive. I would say, have you checked the price of competitive models lately? The pricing between GM, Ford, and Chrysler vehicles and the price for comparative Honda, Toyota, Nissan, and Hyundai models is akin to the difference between Republicans and Democrats: there is not ten cents worth of difference.

Yet foreign brands use non-union labor. These brands are all transplant companies that brought back American jobs but also lower wages to the American segment. Again, with so much of America's economy based on the automobile industry, our beloved Congress only danced to the tune being played by the corporate world.

As the title of this book, *Imperfect Partners*, implies, Congresses going back some forty or more years has mainly shown taking care of special interest: big donors.

During the congressional debate of December 2008, whether to bail out the big three—GM in particular—a news article came out saying this: GM is going strong, just not in the USA. This is consistent with what many have held in belief for a long time. They have been taking billions in USA profits over many years and investing in foreign operations with much success.

This is not a bad thing in itself, and as GM began to become a multinational company, the means for managing should have been adjusted to global conditions simultaneously. In short, the question deserved more scrutinizing than it was given: should we the people have bailed out GM?

There is only ten cents worth of difference between the Republican and the Democratic parties. Until they develop a bipartisan realization that they must recommit the function of their offices to the citizens with equal affection they have had for the corporations, then there may be a possibility to bring back the middle class to make America work again.

"If someone as blessed as I am is not willing to clean out the barn, who will?" (Ross Perot).

Americans have slowly but surely over the past thirty-odd years become frustrated with the position we find ourselves in. It is difficult to project how many millions of middle-class Americans would be giving back to America if our leadership had focused on protecting our manufacturing-based economy versus shrinking it.

The middle class has been reduced so dramatically, without doubt they qualify as an endangered species. They were the sea of souls who, through taxes, financed the roads, bridges, social security, Medicare, Medicaid, etc., all enacted after the Great Depression. The socialized safety net programs and brick-and-mortar infrastructure of America, if you will.

The middle class is the stalwart workhorses that pulled the load for the country and lifted the heavy burden from the poor. The corporations attempt to take credit for being taxed to death, and they may have been, but the really big corporations also found a way to avoid those high taxes implementing escapism and reinvestment or acquisition.

The record shows that many of them pay no taxes at all. Politicians may have gained the praise of we the people by imposing those high taxes on corporate America. At the same time, they gave the corporate world a free pass to defund America by legislatively doing nothing to discourage them from foreign production and reimporting their own foreign-made products.

Americans and the working poor in particular are not angry about the new global economy. They are angry because they politically have been left out, crossed off, and run over. Not only have their interests been ignored, but also they have not seen any attempts to protect the elements of our economy that are of a vital concern to them and should be a vital concern for our national security.

For millions of middle-class workers, trickle-down economics was the opportunity to reach their highest potential. There was a time when trickle-down economics did work, and quite well at that. That time was when the USA was still a number-one manufacturing nation. Trickle down ended with the export of our manufacturing base to lesser nations.

It is shameful that well into the 90s the buying power of the working class remained the same as 1972 adjusting for inflation.

To think the Iraq invasion was mismanaged pales in comparison to the incompetent management of the White House under several presidents and all sitting Congresses going back a generation.

When you look back over the working years of the whole baby boomer generation, consider how they have been politically and economically victimized, and apply proper definition to what took place, labeling it as political and economic terrorism is not nearly as overstating it as you may think. When you take the time to understand and fully assign responsibility and outcome, you have to ask yourself, "Where was our leadership in this country?"

All Work Is of Value

Factory work is not for everyone, although our history records that industry was and remains the basic (backbone) upon which much technology and high-end peripheral jobs are created in financing, marketing, administration, engineering, patent or copyright, scientific or intellectual properties etc.

China would not have become an economic threat advancing in all the above without first welcoming American investment in gaining a manufacturing foothold.

Back When America Speeds Up

When America began to manufacture, it begot the need to supply its own appetite for goods and services and the means to move products and people in an ongoing litany of improved modernization. America was actually an emerging economy that many, if not most of my readers of *Imperfect Partners*, will find it difficult to imagine that time in history.

We know that when we put up a building, build a dam, extend a rail system, install more and update equipment, we are laying the groundwork or laying the foundation on which something of substance can be built, to sustain generational growth and economic prosperity for future generations to expand and improve upon.

Our economy cannot be based on insurance companies, communications services, administrative agencies, advertising etc. While these sectors may be hot, they are elusively transient at best and dependent at least upon the brick and mortar of business. It is one thing to be a real estate agent; it is another to be a real estate builder.

On the Road to a Welfare State: Beginning with the Rebuilding of Japan

As foreign-product quality began to take on a resemblance to that of those made in America, the direction American workers were headed could be forecasted as accurately as our weather using Satellite Dual Doppler radar. But just because other people in distant lands became resourceful and ingenuous is not the real reason why America now struggles in raising the capital to meet fiscal obligations.

Japan seriously took the ideal of protecting its citizenry against imported products and didn't think twice about putting nationalism ahead of free trade. The USA imports on a year-in and year-out basis are twice as much in dollar value as we export to Japan. There is not one nation on earth that the USA exports more to than we import from. This appears to have been the economic policy the USA has adopted for decades. It has proven to work very well for American investors being assured that they could have American Congresses make free trade easier.

In 2008, John McCain said, "I will stand by your side, not in your way."

The foregoing paragraph is important because it is the classic setup of the global economy. If anyone believes those words are meant for we the people, I believe they would be wrong. I cannot see that phrase having any serious meaning for we the people. Was it intended for the lobbyist quietly and inconspicuously standing at the back of the room, giving representatives with like-minded policies of a free-for-all globalization similar to Senator McCain's that old familiar thumbs-up?

It was absurd for Clinton to stand behind the podium and tell absolute lies about how important our trade relationship is with China when, in fact, we were losing both jobs and wealth. It was contradictory for John McCain to favor imposing sanctions against China in 2000 if they were to be caught selling WMDs (weapons of mass destruction). But then again, in 2008, he believes in engaging with China. It couldn't be because he was running for president—could it?

Strike Up the Band

Conversely, whether it was Bill Clinton, George W. Bush, or hopeful John McCain, none have a problem engaging with China. I think it has a little bit to do with how embedded American corporations are manufacturing in China and exporting to the USA. Neither Clinton, Bush, Nor McCain showed any concern with addressing our out-of-control trade deficit that might upset corporate campaign financing for their own political endeavors.

Again, it matters little which party you believe will represent working people the most or the best. Big politics is most interested in taking care of those who take care of them financially: the corporations who are deeply imbedded globally.

Certain advantages are granted in the "most favored nation clause." You may be saying, "So what? What's the big deal?"

Well, here's the big deal. It gives China specific trade advantages, and then we have the WTO, of which China is a member, that has been authorized and has been given the power to overrule domestic laws of participating nations. Say what?

Bill must have thought the hundreds of thousands of American workers who have lost high-paying jobs to low-cost Chinese workers was impressive to report the following:

Opening statement at a news conference, Washington, DC, May 26, 1994.

Bill Clinton

"Over $8 billion of US exports to China last year supported over 150,000 American jobs," said former president Bill Clinton.

There is a minor problem with former president Clinton's stimulating report. He failed to include that at the same time (1994) China exported to the USA $38.781 billion. So the paltry $8 billion that the USA sent to China represents a US trade deficit of $29.494 billion. There was no 150,000 jobs to support, considering the deficit; those supposed jobs are nonexistent. As Paul Harvey would say, "And that's the rest of the story."

You really cannot say Bill was lying. What he said may have been true within itself. Bill was good at making claims, as you may remember. This is only pocket change to what comes next. Read on.

You are getting close to what the record really shows. Read on.

Economic Policy Institute

http://www.epi.org/publications/entry/bp188/

Costly Trade with China: Millions of US Jobs Displaced with Net Job Loss in Every State by Robert E. Scott.

See media kit.

Contrary to the predictions of its supporters, China's entry into the World Trade Organization (WTO) has failed to reduce its trade surplus with the United States or increase overall US employment. The rise in the US trade deficit with China between 1997 and 2006 has displaced production that could have supported 2,166,000 US jobs.

Most of these jobs (1.8 million) have been lost since China entered the WTO in 2001. Between 1997 and 2001, growing trade deficits displaced an average of 101,000 jobs per year, or slightly more than the total employment in Manchester, New Hampshire.

Since China entered the WTO in 2001, job losses increased to an average of 353,000 per year—more than the total employment in greater Akron, Ohio. Between 2001 and 2006, jobs were displaced in every state and the District of Columbia. Nearly three-quarters of the jobs displaced were in manufacturing industries. Simply put, the promised benefits of trade liberalization with China have been unfulfilled.

Even more simply put, we now have over twenty years of results 1988–2009 to evaluate. Are you as dismayed as I am as to how our leadership can continue to endorse more of the same trade policies that literally are ruining America?

The rise in the US trade deficit with China between 1997 and 2006 has displaced production that could have supported 2,166,000 US jobs.

Thanks to the functional purpose of the WTO, whose purpose is to "ensure that trade flows as smoothly, predictably and freely as possible." Is it that we the people simply do not understand how economics is supposed to work, or is it that we the people understand all too well what is happening to us as we continue the downhill slide, while the multi-national corporations reap the benefits of "smooth, predictable, and free trade made ever more easily"? There is no better system in the world than free trade, so they say.

Who really runs the WTO? Based upon results of imbedded corporate interest in doing business in China getting a lion's share of export business, it seems logical to suspect the multinationals are getting what they want.

With the demise of the middle class, it is much harder to convince the majority of Americans that the free-market system only amounts to the occupation forces attempting to convince us that they are ensuring a free world.

In spite of the dismal results of twenty years of gathered statistics that show a much-different picture for we the people versus the corporations, politicians remain committed to propping up failed policies, ignoring responsibility to the people and handing it over to agencies like the WTO and the United Nations, and hoping that they can get away with incompetent management of the people's affairs in a global sense.

As you hear, see, and review the evidence, you decide for yourself. How do you rate the performance of the WTO, and also that of the UN in the scheme of the global economy and world peace?

Like it or hate it, some degree of socialism is here to stay. Who are the biggest benefactors of socialism? American corporations enjoy the benefits of subsidies from we the people and bailouts when needed.

Subsidies, research, and bailouts footed by taxpayer monies. Sounds like socialism to me no matter what you may call it.

Is There a Proper Place for Socialism in America?

Corporate America continues to cut or cancel employee fringe benefits programs. They also want to throw more and more of the cost for health care on the backs of employees as well. While larger companies are still involved with providing these coverages, they are assuming less and less of a role in these systems.

What does all this mean to we the people? Are we being ushered into a new era of being self-insured? If this is a feature of some grand plan, it appears that no one has worked out the details.

When universal health care is mentioned, the immediate response by those opposed is the astronomical cost over a ten-year period. I have to ask, why are our lawmakers looking at a ten-year period versus comparing how much we the people are spending over a one-year period under our present system and multiplying by 10? Somehow, it makes me feel like I am not being given accurate comparison statistics.

I get the feeling that real numbers are being maximized and real answers are being avoided while our focus and attention is being drawn into meaningless discussion.

What is really important and concerns most Americans is the cost of health care. Presently, a catastrophic or chronic health condition can leave a person bankrupt. It's the cost that matters.

"If you like your doctor, you should be able to keep your doctor." "If you like your present insurance plan, you should be able to keep your plan."

These elements are all very true, real and important issues. Those who oppose a universal plan emphasize choice as a harbinger for rejecting a socialized system. Choice in one's doctor and choice where or at what hospital are important. It is much about coverage and cost. Choice in keeping one's present plan would be abandoned rather quickly if an equal or better plan was offered at a lower—cost period.

Corporate America is abandoning their former role in providing both retirement and health care programs, even with what I assume amounts to huge tax write-offs from the States or Washington. The question is, can we the people do better for ourselves than what employers are no longer able or willing to provide as fringe benefits?

Presently, Social Security, Medicare, and Medicaid are self-insured programs. Have you ever considered what we the people are now spending for profit coverages? In the private sector, a health care plan costs in excess of $10,000 per year for a plan that really only addresses catastrophic illnesses, not covering out-of-pocket co-pays, deductibles, etc.

Seniors are paying out of pocket $200 to $500 per person per month for supplemental Medicare plans that are being bought from private insurance companies. The $200/$500 per month represents $2,400 to $6,000 per year just to defray the 20 percent that Medicare does not cover. That is quite a chunk of change for an individual or a senior couple whose primary income may be social security. I believe that insurance companies really do like the system just the way it is.

In light of the tremendous amount of money we Americans now dole out to insurance companies in terms of premiums, deductibles, and co-pays in an effort to ward off possible financial ruin due to chronic conditions, accident, or illness. Can we do better by diverting those same monies that we now hand over to the for-profit insurance companies, and do a better job of securing better health care for ourselves, cutting out the middleman (insurance companies)? The single important question to this complex issue is this: can we do better and at overall lower cost? Cost is at a crisis level and has to be overcome.

Our congressmen or congresswomen are well cared for in health, sickness, and retirement.

They have admitted that every American should have access to the same level of health care that they do. It has been said, and most people agree, that health care should be viewed as a civil rights issue. As it now stands, we the people only enjoy the level of health care that we can afford.

By, for, and of the People

If there is any single economic or political model that can claim superiority in every aspect, the USA is and has been since 1930 easily defined as partly Democratic and partly Socialistic. The question is, what will it take to make our Constitution work the way it is supposed to? Our nation is going to have to endure a true cultural change like nothing before in the way we utilize our resources and our collective relationships around the globe.

I have spoken about Ross Perot and how he, if elected to the presidency, intended to "clean out the barn," look out for America first, and spend our money prudently. I am prompted to believe that Ross Perot was indeed a person before his time. But America wasn't ready for someone like him yet.

An Era of Social Modernization

In 1935, the UAW advocated for a national tax-funded health insurance plan to protect working families from the financial ruin an unforeseen medical emergency could bring. During and after World War II, the unions supported various efforts by Congress and President Truman to create such a system, but the AMA and private insurers defeated all such proposals. The UAW turned to the bargaining table to address the growing problem of rapidly rising health care costs.

When General Motors refused to bargain over medical benefits, the UAW filed unfair-labor-practice charges with the National Labor Relations Board. The board upheld the union's position, and in the 1950 negotiations, GM agreed to pay half the cost of hospital and surgical coverage for its workers and their family members.

Ford and Chrysler fell in pattern the same year. By 1954, almost all UAW members and their families had health care coverage for hospitalization, surgery, office visits, and other treatments, with the companies paying half the insurance costs.

And so it was an era of extensive achievement for the UAW and their families. Remember during that time period: "So goes the big three, so goes the rest of the country."

"So goes the big three, so goes the nation." In that era, the unions were so powerful that all eyes were on Detroit and the auto and trucking business under the leadership of Walter Reuther and James "Jimmy" Hoffa.

Most public service workers were not unionized at that time; however, their legislative bodies looked closely at what Detroit was negotiating, and while they could not match the pay rate that federal, state, and municipalities made up in fringe benefits such as health care, vacation or sick time, and early-retirement options.

As I have stated, public servants could spend more time at the water cooler without hindering their overall productivity. Those who worked on assembly lines were not afforded such working-conditions luxuries, and hence, that is why production line workers were paid more. As history records, that would change.

Source: http://www.uaw.org/history/uaw70years.html

Those were the days, my friend. They thought they would never end.

Unions were strong, and even the National Labor Relations Board respected the UAW. But those days are gone, and rarely does the NLRB rule in favor of labor. The new global economy is holding the big stick for anti-labor forces, specifically the WTO and the UN. Have been dominate anti workers' rights and aligned themselves with the corporations in maintaining low wages, especially in third-world nations. Why so much emphasis on emerging nation economies? Again, that is where the greater opportunities exist for the multinationals.

Desperate Financing

There was no other good reason for lotteries except they were a quick and easy cash cow to make up for exporting America's treasure once held in our manufacturing base.

What does the implementation of lotteries indicate? Maybe nothing to many people, and maybe a lot to people who are opposed to the lure of gambling by those deemed least able to afford it. There is much controversy surrounding lotteries as to whether it is in reality just another tax.

Whatever your personal position may be on this matter is your choice. It is probably worthy to take note as to the timing of *when* lotteries began to catch on. Is it coincidental that they became very popular at the same time tax monies were being lost primarily because of American manufacturing being taken offshore?

This writer strongly believes that lotteries were the end run to make up for lost revenue directly tied to our very own Congresses' failure to do their job of managing international trade. Could this tactic be akin to adding insult to injury to America's working people? First, Congress allowed and encouraged jobs and treasure to leave our shores and then replace lost tax monies with gambling that is patronized by those least able to afford it.

Would it be unfair to even suggest that it is conceivable that many desperate states adopted the lottery as their economic readjustment plan? Nonetheless, there is only one way to describe what was taking place across America: de-capitalization.

When citizens become de-capitalized, it puts in motion the domino effect that moves so quickly it is difficult to tell who gets toppled first and last. However, when the working people lose, everyone loses—town, county, state, and federal.

Now isn't it strange that Washington doesn't seem to understand what they can do to stem the tide of such cataclysmic financial erosion?

Ellis Island is a symbol of America's immigrant heritage. From 1892 to 1954, this immigrant depot processed the greatest tide of incoming humanity in the nation's history. Nearly twelve million landed here in their search of freedom of speech and religion, and for economic opportunity.

For Those Entering the Workforce in the 1970s

They experienced the brunt of the whipsaw effect of layoffs, transfers, and job changing.

Retraining was more of a failure than a success from the standpoint that the economy in many areas was stagnant to begin with. From the sharp exodus of American jobs, many seasoned workers were competing with junior people holding degrees applying for jobs that even they were overqualified for.

With what residue of manufacturing we did retain, along with the inventive spirit that made America great the first time around did show our best side in developing technology intellectual properties and services. We managed to do exceedingly well under the circumstances in which we found ourselves in.

Silicon Valley served as a holy land and savior for America in a time of desperate economic revival.

Those who said in the 60s that the USA would become a services society were right. If it wasn't for the fast-paced development of electronics, and the computer in particular, we would not have any definable economy unless consumerization qualifies.

The January 1977 edition of *Popular Electronics* featured the Altair 8800 computer kit, based on Intel's 8080 microprocessor, on its cover. Within weeks of the computer's debut, customers inundated the manufacturing company, MITS, with orders. Bill Gates and Paul Allen licensed BASIC as the software language for the Altair. Ed Roberts invented the 8800, which sold for $297, or $395 with a case, and coined the term "personal computer."

Finding Ways to Cope

We truly were living up to the prophecy made in the 1960s about becoming a services-oriented economy. Welcome the laptop, notebook, smartphone, online business, and on and on.

On your next visit to Walmart, if you see a greeter that looks like they may have retired once before or should have been retired long ago, there is a good possibility that they are the recipients of a company that did such a good job of holding the line on costs, or making sure we competed with foreign workers. That is why they are there, to supplement the retirement that never came in. Yes, there are a few that just want to work for something to do.

Introducing the lottery system to shore up state revenues is not a very embraceable economic readjustment plan, any more than implementing a retraining work program for middle-aged workers to compete in a declining work environment.

So You Think War on the Middle Class Is a Harsh Statement? Read On

As recent as October 2007, the National Council of Agricultural Employers has asked the Bush administration to "hasten the Visa process to ease housing requirements for workers, lower the required wage for such labor and *expand the list of tasks* they are allowed to do."

"Grower groups would also like the administration to create a path to citizenship for many undocumented farm workers."

The Labor Department carried out their marching orders to the letter. Of course the way it is written in a complex or condensed manner (i.e., dividing the country into 530 areas and pay wages appropriately will leave anyone in the dark as to what is going to take place in the field). They are exceptionally good at creating smoke.

By JESSE J. HOLLAND, AP
05 February 2008 @ 08:05 pm EST

Changes Aimed at Foreign Farm Worker Pay
The Labor Department planned Wednesday to propose changes to the foreign agriculture worker program, among

them how the base wages for H2-A visa holders are determined. Streamlining the hiring process for H2-A visa holders could help turn employers away from hiring illegal workers, officials said.

Right now, the base pay for H2-A agriculture workers is set by the Agriculture Department's Farm Labor Survey and varies by state. Within a state, the pay is the same regardless of what job a worker performs.

The Change

However, the Labor Department wants to use the Bureau of Labor Statistic's Occupational Employment Survey, which would allow officials to consider what workers do and their skill levels. It also would allow officials to divide the country into more than 530 areas and to pay wages appropriate to each area.

"Because of the increased precision, there are going to be wages that will likely decrease," said Leon R. Sequeira, an assistant secretary for policy at the Labor Department. "There also are wages that are going to increase."

http://www.ibtimes.com/articles/20080205/changes-aimed-at-foreign-farm-worker-pay.htm

In January, 2009. US District judge Ricardo M. Urbina refused the request from the United Farm Workers and Farmworker Justice to stop the Labor Department from instituting new H2-A visa rules.

Associated Press
January 15, 2009

WASHINGTON—A federal judge on Thursday (turned down) a request to stop the Bush administration from instituting new rules that will make it easier for farmers to bring in foreign work crews to harvest their spring crops.

U.S. District Judge Ricardo M. Urbina refused the request from the United Farm Workers and Farmworker Justice to stop the Labor Department from instituting new H2-A visa rules.

H2-A visas are used by the agriculture industry to hire temporary farm workers.

The groups had argued that the Bush administration's overhaul of the country's agricultural worker program would lower wages in the fields, erode labor protections and make it EASIER FOR CONTRACTORS TO BYPASS HIRING LEGAL U.S. WORKERS.

Please note: "Make is easier to bypass hiring legal US workers."

What is the opposite of *legal*? *Illegal*, is it not? Unless I am misinterpreting this statement, it looks like George W. Bush is nodding to illegal immigration and also instituting a (formula) to lower wages to boot.

But District Judge Urbina said they did not present enough proof that their members would "suffer immediate decreased wages, increased transportation costs, or loss of employment."

The new rules go into effect Saturday, (only days) before the Bush administration leaves office.

http://www.foreignlaborcert.doleta.gov/h-2a.cfm

Regardless of how George W. Bush portrays himself as being disliked by immigrants, they've got to love him for his desire to make illegal border crossing possible for all of them that he possibly can. George is saying the right thing, though, about legal immigrants not liking him. Why should they? He is striking at their very livelihood.

Do you see that George W. Bush and District Judge Urbina are peas in a pod favoring illegal migrants? George

W. Bush may wear the label of a conservative on his sleeve, but he sure wears the liberal label when it comes to giving a hand up to illegals.

Corporate farmers are constituents that most likely line up in his receiving line. George W. Bush was able to accomplish this only days before leaving office on January 20, 2009. I am willing to wager that George W. Bush will get some handsome leaving-office gifts and bonuses from this final act.

The United Farm Workers are actually in a better position than the UAW—if they can hold their members together. Their option is to call a strike and make sure every worker honors their picket lines. That is the way early American unions were able to get bargaining power with employers. Obviously, with exporting jobs, it rendered formerly powerful unions powerless. But that is not the case with food growers—those crops must be picked.

Can you see the opportunity for blurring what H2-A/B cardholders actually are able to do once they are in the United States? I have underlined the word *contractors* in this report. On one hand, employers are referred to as farmers and, in the same breath, contractors. When it comes down to what tasks, the H2-A/B will amount to the same difference as between Republicans and Democrats.

H1-B Visa Holders

Even in the high-tech economy, the search is on for professional workers whose standard of living is well below ours. Other factors such as climate and culture contribute to their cost of living being much less. Corporations are finding that they can recruit professional workers for as little as one-third that of Americans.

Have you walked down the halls of your local hospital meeting a contingent of medical staff lately, and noticed the diversity? It is difficult to believe we have such a shortage of people entering the medical field. Are these also "jobs that Americans are unwilling to do"?

It has been argued that US scientists are not in short supply as claimed, yet many scientists are immigrating into the USA. Will this be the beginning of still-more contention on global economy issues? I completely do realize that immigrating scientists are looking for the best opportunity to capture the good life that they have worked hard to educate themselves.

Having said that, why then is their only opportunity in immigrating? Could it be that if we took a deeper look at their country's economy, we can see that it is being held back by corporations engaged in developing their primitive society by bringing in investment and offering those already discussed competitive wages?

The continuous and constant changing way the global economy produces, distributes, and consumes goods and services can no longer afford to be left to the will of corporations that take as much as they can and give back as little as possible. The top 2 percent who reside at the corporate level are controlling who becomes a millionaire and who becomes a billionaire. After that, Mom and Pop, who have a little savings invested in Wall Street's stock market, may get a small ROA or ROI, whether you want to call it assets or investment. They will be fortunate if a market adjustment doesn't wipe away their expectations for a secure financial future.

Commerce throughout the world cannot continue to afford the disruptive volatility to our financial, social, and productive systems simply to satisfy the selfish ambitions of the rich investors (tossing loaded dice). War on the middle class as this economic fiasco has been labeled, and will only worsen without intelligent, responsible intervention.

As you continue to read on in *Imperfect Partners*, the more you will see how our economy got to be in the mess it is. Action is needed to restore a semblance of balance that restores commensurate wages and salaries and a more predictable or secure investment growth for the rank and file.

It is widely agreed to that many of the elite actually earn only a fraction of outlandish awards presently granted to them. As I have repeatedly stated in different ways, our systems cannot run like a rudderless wind-driven ship. Very few things are completely free, and to leave the global economy to its own devices without better management intervention is nothing short of irresponsible, reactionary leadership at the helm.

The richest 2 percent of adults in the world own more than half of all household wealth, according to a new study by a United Nations research institute.

The report, from the World Institute for Development Economics Research at the UN University, says that the poorer half of the world's population own barely 1 percent of global wealth.

Internationally Speaking

The interesting thing about this report from the UN University is that after reviewing the aims of the UN charter, it is clear that one thing they do (maybe the only thing they do) is develop reports. Having been in existence since 1945, they should have something to show for we the people in fulfilling their purposes.

Concerning the accomplishments of the UN, are we supposed to appreciate what we cannot see, or should we be able to see something that we can appreciate? As I have said, I cannot see enough accomplishment of the United Nations Organization to qualify their existence.

The Bureau of Labor Statistics and the Labor Department are precision workers. They have made that claim. "Because of the increased precision," and the way they are going to divide the country into 530 areas. They are good when it comes to pushing those who are down, down even further.

We the people are unable to bring our health care crisis under control for lack of precision management. More precisely, we cannot seem to even make our health care system manageable.

It is strange how government can get things done when the benefits are going in a selected direction. Their use of precision in dividing the country into areas to set wages of migrant workers more precisely is really quite hysterical.

Shhh! Someone Might Be Listening

For those of you who remember, it was the ambition of Hilary Clinton in 1994 to bring reform to the health care system. It was one of the strangest events how she announced her intentions (shortly after Bill's second term), and then there was silence.

Yes, silence. I do not recall the media interviewing her or newspaper accounts or television airings. I never was able to understand why she went from advocate to disinterested so quickly. But I've got a pretty good idea what was behind her silence until 2008. It had to be the insurance companies. I am as positive about this as anything I have ever been positive about. I believe they (the insurance industry) told her, in no uncertain terms, "Sit down and shut up."

There is always the possibility that through further research and consideration she changed her mind. If so, she did not clarify it that I ever recall.

Depending on the myriad of polls taken, it is difficult to know what percentage of Americans want a public wholly owned universal health care system. It is pretty accurate to state, though, that between 50 and 75 percent of Americans are between dissatisfied and very dissatisfied with our present system. That dissatisfaction is predominately driven by costs. It is costs for premiums and the cost of treatment equally. Let me submit the following for your consideration.

Insurance premiums are out of sight because treatment costs are so ridiculously high that it is bankrupting the system. Where does most of the billing come from? The hospitals. In many cases, the physicians and specialists only work for the hospital. That indicates to me that hospitals are corporate entities. As such, they are behind what it costs for you or me to be hospitalized, treated, and released.

Thirty thousand dollars or more is not uncommon for a heart catheterization, stent, and exit within twenty-four hours. This is an example of the more-modest cost treatments. There is a lot of cloudiness surrounding hospitals' functionality and their relationship to the political system.

It appears that the public would be open to any kind of a plan as long as it reduced personal costs, improved access and quality of care.

When GM and Chrysler were reorganizing, the UAW wanted the government to come forward with a public-owned system.

It has been reported that America is not ready for true universal health care. Is that a reality, a ruse, or a reason for the politicians to pursue everything except a public health care system? Universal health care has been an issue since 1935, when Franklin Roosevelt tried to make it a part of the New Deal.

Critics of universal health care contend that all the advanced strides, inventions, procedures, etc., are the result of a free-market, competitive, for-profit system. Proponents claim that only a free-market system is able to motivate those in the industry.

Research to gain knowledge and invent new improved medicines, devices, and treatment for disease to help people live full lives in the best health possible can be achieved only by employing the inspirational system. They believe that limiting profits or setting parameters as to what practitioners can charge will diminish the motivation of research and practitioners to enter the medical research and health care services, thereby causing a decline in the quality of our health care system.

Concerning this philosophy, I will offer the following thought. My first thought is our present system amounts to a license to steal, and second, why does the USA rank thirty-seventh among all other nations in quality?

Health Care

The USA ranked thirty-seventh. "Unlike most of the nations commended by WHO, the United States doesn't have one comprehensive health system, noted Dr. Crone. "Instead, we have multiple microsystems."

Life Expectancy

"The United States rated twenty-fourth under this system, or an average of 70.0 years of healthy life for babies born in 1999."

"Basically, you die earlier and spend more time disabled if you're an American rather than a member of most other advanced countries."

How many of the corporate insurance, pharmaceutical, and medical appliance companies have their hand out to Uncle Sam for grants, gifts from agencies, organizations, foundations, etc., rather than use their exorbitant profits to do research, invent new devices, medicines, and, lastly, causes for a cure come knocking at our doors for donations?

Yes, indeed, they tout the free-market system at the same time enjoying socialism at its finest. Is this a case of having your cake and eating it too?

What Does Less Government Really Mean?

Most Americans are quick to agree that less government is in their best interest, and in a few cases, it is. Mom and pop-size businesses will give bureaucracy as a reason for going out of business. So where do we see more-, less-, or right-size government actually taking place? The investment and banking sectors are the biggies!

Wall Street investors and the banking institutions both whine for the government to unchain them. What happened under the George W. Bush administration when the rules were relaxed? Most of us know what happened with worthless securities, toxic assets, fraudulent balance sheets, CEO salaries, loan forgiveness, exorbitant bonuses for top executives.

The sad fact is that in all the time since there has been talk of clamping down and imposing more regulations so we could once again say, "We need to make sure this never happens again." Does that sound familiar? The second sad fact is that no matter who is in the White House, the big bosses on the Street seem to be more in control than the White House or Congress. Right-size government seems unattainable.

Who Says Terrorism Comes in Only One Form?

The acts committed by Wall Street professionals directly caused the 2008 collapse that took down our global financial system. The result has been on par with a terrorist attack, and what are we doing to bring the perps to justice?

As last reported, many high-ranking financiers were asked to make recommendations to Congress what could be done to avert another such meltdown. As of a late report, Tim Geithner was not in favor of putting any limits on top executive salaries or bonuses. It is very close to bringing in a bank robber to advise on how to avoid bank robberies, thanking the perp, and calling him a taxi.

There are a few who have said Wall Street should be able to regulate themselves. They are probably correct in making that assumption; however, the record demonstrates that Wall Street has too many electronic tools that make corrupt practices easier for Wall Streeters to cheat the system.

I am of the opinion that when there is a market correction, not only do they survive but also they thrive. In short, they have access to advanced tools of the trade, along with reliable insider information, which means they make money in a bull or a bear market.

Does all the shady dealings of Wall Street mean that the rest of us finance their profit taking? I think it does.

The *Post* said President Barack Obama's administration believes it can sidestep the rules because it has, in many cases, decided not to provide federal aid directly to the financial institutions, instead setting up special entities that act as middlemen to channel the funds. It smells like socialism to me, folks.

As you will hear me say often, there is only ten cents worth of difference between the Democrats and the Republicans when it comes right down to it. For Obama to follow Geithner's lead to do this puts his administration right in goose step with the Bush administration before him.

What's Education Got to Do with It?

Only when it became apparent that corporations would use the opportunity to import skilled workers, including scientists, from poorer nations at much-lower salaries did universities and other institutions of advanced learning become concerned about the impact this practice could have now that it included them. This type of labor forces (utilization) is the business model that the sociopolitical science universities fully supported throughout the 60s, 70s, and only beginning in the 1990s has there been a marked turnaround in their public stance.

What can we draw from their change in attitude? Apparently they did not see the day coming when the long arm of globalization and technology would reach out and up to those who thought they were untouchable.

The multi-national corporations have more to do with the running of the USA and every nation on planet Earth than we can imagine. Are we indeed being governed by corporate communism and not even realize it?

As an average American, you may be wondering what our universities and other institutions of advanced learning have to do with or influence foreign and domestic economic policies. Well, that is where all politicians and corporate executives are groomed. Secondly, most have deep roots with their alma mater. And thirdly, these institutions are where much of the research studies and statistical data is collected for corporate and governmental use.

It makes it much easier to see how there is a mad scramble to make it into the top 2 percent where the really big money is, and everyone below that level falls into the category of labor as a commodity to now include the fairly well educated. It is just another sign of small steps working up to the new world order through globalism.

Just how deep of a relationship exists between our universities, corporations, and the political establishment?

Corporations and Alumni who have made the big time after graduation both frequently establish endowments that outpace anything they willingly give to their localities or to Uncle Sam in the form of taxes, etc.

As Leona Helmsley—wife of real estate tycoon Harry Helmsley, long remembered for her brash personality—once said, "Only little people pay taxes." Can we believe she meant what she said? Maybe she meant big people do not pay taxes, they only pay dues. If they have connections, *have people*, and keep up their dues, *the club* will see to it that they are taken care of.

Does this mean that all corporations are run by immoral and unethical people? Obviously not. However, what we do see and what we need to fully understand and to hold in all diligence is opportunity. When power, position, and opportunity are catalyzed by access to money, it invariably will bring out the worst in those who are easily corrupted by power and position.

Corporate-Owned Media

We the people usually have high regard for members of the news media (personnel or personalities). Mass media is almost universally the mechanism through which we the people receive information for the basis of much of what we believe in, how it influences our daily living, how we make important decisions, and even how we plan our futures.

Media brings us current events as well as historical facts. They also keep us abreast on the political and economic climate. In general, one may conclude that we turn on our media devices to get a daily briefing to update our social, mental, and spiritual mentality.

Are we supposed to believe everything that we see and hear through the media, or do some of them also have a pony in the show? Should we the people veer to the safe side in how much trust we place in some media reporting, as they too are owned by corporations? Corporations have selected political candidates they want given top billing and those they want second rated.

Do you think it is difficult to control what reporters report? Let me make it simple: they know which side their bread is buttered on, for instance.

Meredith Vieira most likely would be a little uncomfortable discussing such things at length. It was reported that "Meredith Vieira, was (molding) the reported $10 million a year job to fit her lifestyle as she prepared to join co-host Matt Lauer on 'Today.'

Day after Day, They Stump for Middle America

Other than corporate Fox News and a very few journalism mavericks such as CNN's Lou Dobbs and Jack Cafferty, who have mounted the crusade for the working class at least they appear to be a voice for the struggling average American, there are thousands of reporters but only a handful of crusaders.

Birds of a Feather Do Flock Together

When the corporations were eyeing foreign labor markets to replace American labor, many of the political science-oriented universities were joined at the hip with them on free-trade agreements. Why wouldn't they be? They had all things in common.

Labor had come to mean different things to different people. It has often been said labor was and is something that is to be bought and sold in the free market, and nothing more. If it sounds callous, cold, and indifferent, that is exactly what it really is in the new global economy.

Why would the most important resource (people) to this entire concept be regarded with outright contempt? Who really believes the corporate phraseology? "People are our most important resource"? Yes, not all are this callous.

Aren't the men, women, and—yes—children who make the global economy go round and round more important than empty meaningless words? If we truly had government by, for, and of the people, we would be doing better than this. As Lou Dobbs would say, "Can't we expect government that works?"

Since US leadership will not lead in global trade policies that give American workers equal footing to participate in the global economy, and halt the decline of the American middle class and transfer of American wealth, we the people can only hope and pray that someone with the political will to clean out the barn, as Ross Perot put it, comes along, and the economic environment evolves enough to get him or her elected as it appears that the deep-state old-guard politicians are too corporately entrenched to change on their own.

What Is the Definition of Middle Class?

Friday, January 11, 2008
Taken from an Excerpt
What is the middle class?

Without any firm numbers defining the beginning and end of the middle class, Tess Vigeland checks with experts and the presidential candidates for their definitions.

How much money does it take to be in the middle class?

Well, at least there's an official poverty line. In 2007, it was an annual income under $20,650 for a family of four.

As for middle class, well, the Congressional Research Service issued a report last year pegging middle-class income as between $19,000 a year and $91,000 a year.–

Sounds as if they would rather that we the people remain a little in the dark (or fog) concerning the number of middle-income Americans there are, or are not.

But even the specialist in quantitative economics who put together that study said there is no consensus or official government definition.

So we decided to ask around.

First up: Brookings Institution economist Gary Burtless.

Gary Burtless: "You don't need to show a passport or a baptism certificate or a club ID to be admitted to this group. If you say you're a member, then I think you're in the middle class."

He uses the term "middle income" rather than "middle class," and he bases his definition on the median household income, which last year was $48,200.

Burtless says the middle can range from half of that to twice that number, so $24,000 to $96,000.

But in surveys, people and families far outside that range will say they're middle class. Burless says that's just American egalitarianism at work.

Burtless: "So people who have very high incomes may not want to claim superior position. Similarly, people who have modest incomes do not want to accept any indication that they have second-class status in our society."

MIT economist Frank Levy came up with a definition based on census data for families in their prime earning years.

Frank Levy: "I would say a reasonable range is about $30,000 to $90,000. Most of what we mean by middle class, I think, is how easy it is for you to afford the basic building blocks of a good life in America, and that means can you afford a single-family house, and can you afford a car, and can you afford to heat the house, and so on and so forth."

And finally, we hit the campaign trail to find out how this year's presidential candidates are trying to attract the middle class.

Here's how Republican Mike Huckabee is drawing the line in a current TV ad.

Mike Huckabee: "I believe most Americans want their next president to remind them of the guy they work with, not the guy who laid them off."

Huckabee isn't the only candidate wooing the middle class. John Edwards is well known for his "two Americas" theme. Republicans like John McCain and Rudy Giuliani say their tax-cut proposals will help the middle class, and Hillary Clinton promised not to raise taxes on those making above $97,500 just to save Social Security:

In a recent debate, Barack Obama took issue with that figure:

Barack Obama: "Understand that only 6 percent of Americans make more than $97,000 a year. So, 6 percent is not the middle class, it's the upper class."

And Clinton's response?

Clinton: "It is absolutely the case that there are people who would find that burdensome. I represent firefighters. I represent school supervisors. I'm not talking, I mean, you know...it's different parts of the country."

Exactly. Go to Bankrate.Com's cost-of-living calculator and compare two major cities.

Living a nice life on $90,000 in Atlanta? You'll need $147,000 here in Los Angeles for a similar life.

Ugh.

Source: http://marketplace.publicradio.org/display/web/2008/01/11/what_is_the_middle_class

Was Hillary trying to appeal to a few too many constituents and she got a little tongue tied? (Ugh.)

Hillary is correct, though; the income needed to live in different parts of the country does vary widely. But I think some people choose to play the issue of widely differing so that they can use the latitude to prevent getting themselves boxed in as to where they personally stand on issues. It seems obvious that she didn't want to tax the upper class to fix social security.

So now we don't know much more than before. It looks like the people you would expect to know such things would rather not commit to any standard.

We will have to compromise those figures for a more middle-America number. Common sense tells me that something between $40,000 and $65,000 would represent a greater percentage of middle-class American incomes.

How many millions of American workers are in the ranks of the working poor? My estimate is somewhere around 40 percent of Americans may fit this profile. Forty percent likely are paying little to no federal taxes. If that is anywhere near accurate, is it any wonder that we cannot afford to fix our roads and bridges, meet public budgets, and fulfill entitlement obligations?

Why have I gone to all this trouble attempting to figure out who and how many Americans make up our middle class or middle-income bracket, as Gary Burtless, Brookings Institution economist, uses the term "middle income" rather than "middle class," and he bases his definition on the median household income, which last year was $48,200.

There is a couple of important questions based on what these presidential candidates have said. If only 6 percent of working Americans make more than $97,000 per year and the poverty line is $20,650, with corporations working overtime to drive wages in America from $20 per hour downward, how many Americans are getting closer and closer to the poverty line (as an ongoing campaign)?

Taking into account the millions of American jobs that have gone to foreign lands and how corporate America is more or less forcing what is left of America's middle class to compete with second-world labor force rates through decreased wages etc., etc.

The cash cow middle-income class in America has all but been annihilated. That being said, the middle-income class is where most of the tax monies came from that has kept America's infrastructure afloat throughout our industrial era, pre NAFTA and China joining the WTO.

Do we all see the desperation and lengths every level of government is being compelled to resort to, such as implementing state lotteries as an alternative revenue makeup system?

Some may have the opinion that lotteries were an ingenious idea to make up for the incompetent foreign-trade policies that amounted to economic and political terrorism on American workers. At the same time, they are desperate to continue unaffordable pay raises to public service personnel to appeal for votes to keep themselves in office.

These desperate reactive moves all point back to governmental leadership failure to manage international trade (supporting economic equality principles) versus nodding their heads to appease corporate manufacturers' and investors' quest for free trade made easier.

As you can easily see and determine from Washington's actions and outcome, they created the dire dilemma that has affected the US economy so ruinously.

I chose *Imperfect Partners* as the title of this book to be as fair with our leadership, whose most important duty is to defend our nation from any and all forces that jeopardize life, liberty, and the pursuit of happiness.

It has been overwhelmingly reported that if minimum wages had kept pace with congressional member raises, minimum wages would be about $23 per hour. Ironically, that translates into a yearly income of just about $47,840.

These figures are exactly where I have been able to establish to qualify as middle income or to be regarded as a middle-class American at the time of this writing.

To put it into perspective how the middle-class American was ripped from our economy is just another way to make sense, when we fully recognize that what happened to middle America was quite simply economic and political terrorism.

As Long as Washington Continues to Endorse Economic Poverty Policies, Is There an Alternative?

One of the next best things has been suggested by a senior adviser to President Bill Clinton, a visiting fellow at the Progressive Policy Institute. The unnamed writer said, "On its own, the minimum wage is an imperfect means for ensuring no full-time worker is poor. First, it almost certainly will not be raised enough."

Published statistics for 2004, the most recent year with solid available data, show that about 3.5 million full-time workers earned less than poverty-level wages. Factoring in government benefits, about 2.6 percent of full-time workers live below the poverty line. That is about 2.7 million Americans. And these struggling workers frequently support families, meaning millions more depend on them.

The writer from the Progressive Policy Institute suggests overhauling the EITC (earned income tax credit). He or she says that this is the best time in a decade to make this bargain with low-wage workers. An increased minimum wage will help millions of poor people: combining it with a new commitment to the EITC could take them the rest of the way out of poverty. Arguably, supporting those who are working hard and playing by the rules is as important a societal good as tax breaks for companies, or even (encouraging) home ownership.

"As important a societal good as tax breaks for companies or even encouraging home ownership" is an important statement to understand that the writer at Progressive Policy Institute is making inference that if those who are wealthy enough to qualify for a tax break, then those too poor to qualify should also be entitled to something comparable. From these two scenarios, you can see that there is a lot of room for meaningful debate concerning left-wing economic inequality and right-wing limited resistance to socialism. I have purposely used the term "limited resistance to socialism" by the Republican or conservative faction because they are just as complicit in meting out taxpayer (bailout, grant, etc.) money as the Democratic liberal camp in many instances.

It wasn't the Japanese. It wasn't the Mexicans, and it wasn't the Chinese that started this avalanche of economic decline in the USA. It was American Corporations sucking up to American politicians to take lobbyist gifts and look the other way, while manufacturers unbolted the machinery from the factory floor, loaded up the ships, and sailed away. In effect, could we call this an imperfect partnership of complicity?

Occasionally Cheaters Get Caught

There was a news report of strange activity taking place where many people were observed coming and going from an adobe house in the middle of the Arizona desert. An investigation revealed that out there was some thirty foreign-national computer-programming tech people working for an American firm at one-third the going rate as American programmers.

War on the middle class knows no boundaries. It seems that everywhere we see and hear about big business aberrations, multinational corporations in one way, shape, or form will be found right in the middle of corrupt activity driving poverty policies for workers.

It was recently stated by Barack Obama that "no one should have to leave their hometown to find a world-class job."

(Best of its kind).

BusinessDictionary.com.

The ripple effect is picking up momentum, and how can war on the middle class be managed? This is not a new phenomenon; it has been going on for thirty years, it has merely moved up one rung on the ladder and gotten the attention of our political science students, and it has gotten their attention because they are in the crosshairs of the new global economy.

The answers that this next generation of activists from the political socio-science universities seek are one generation late. If they thought the new global economy would never become a threat to them, they were wrong.

The corporations will be satisfied only when they have driven their labor cost to the lowest common denominator. After all, there is one concern in this business model: profit. I think we would be safe to estimate that there is between 2 and 5 percent of the people who are at the top of the corporations, which are the ones looking out for themselves. When we hear them plead their case about costs, responsibility to shareholders, and bottom line, they make a good, sound argument.

But when you consider that *who* gets the bulk of profits (in the forms of dividends, stock options, bonuses, salaries, perks etc.), what is left over represents less than a level playing field for the small investor (middle class) to get an equitable return on his/her meager IRA, 401, etc., retirement investment.

Corporate leaders often sit on financial institution board of directors and vice versa. Financial institution executives often sit on the board of directors of corporations. This is a cozy relationship that guarantees many very handsome rewards.

If you lost money in a market correction, where do you suppose that paper flew away to? Have you heard the term "controlled explosion," such as used to bring down dilapidated structures to build anew on the old site? Let's face it: many of us, if not most of us, do not have the resources to know just when that explosion or market correction is about to occur. Therefore, we are at the mercy of those with the resources, the knowledge, and the power to not only survive but also thrive in any explosive market condition, planned or unplanned.

I don't have any concrete proof for what I have described as a market correction explosion, but neither have I ever heard of big-time investors like Mike Bloomberg, Warren Buffett, or John Paulson losing money in the market. The rich do indeed get richer, and the poor do indeed struggle.

Advance Technology Is Not All Bad for Workers

Because of the advances in technology, the need for more employees is often no longer required. This makes the philosophy of trickle-down economics just about as obsolete as bell-bottom pants. However, there is somewhat of a silver lining to robots versus human hand. Increased productivity and maintenance spell higher pay for those needed to keep production lines running and increased profits for the manufacturers.

Remember the story of the young boy with his shiny new jackknife whittling a green sapling?

Our free-market politics are giving big-hitter foreign automakers advantages that even American companies do not have. There is a very visible reason behind this anomaly. Our political establishment squandered or whittled our manufacturing capacity down to such low levels that we are now desperate to bring some of our once-greatness back.

Our desperation warrants that our politicians get on their knees and beg foreign competitors Toyota, Honda,

Nissan, Hyundai, Volkswagen, and other equipment makers to set up shop on our home turf. They are getting political green lights, tax breaks, and bypassing union labor as an incentive to come.

We cannot fault foreign investors for exercising good business sense. They understand the benefit of production at the point of consumption, and seeing that the Japanese standard of living is paralleling with ours, it makes sense to locate here.

As a side issue in this our Congress not only gave the imports great breaks to bring back jobs but also set a precedent non-union labor that severed the bargaining power of the UAW at Chrysler, GM, and Ford. Yes, indeed, they would be working for less as well.

Some would hail this major industry overhaul as a market correction. I have heard it said that UAW workers were making too much in wages anyway. If that is the case, I have to ask, what about the millions of public service workers who continue to be doing much better, as so stated in research media? Oh, yes, the politicians negotiate their total benefits packages, and yes, public service workers do vote.

"And that's the rest of the story."

The WTO Is an Anti-Worker Organization: Read It Next

World Trade Organization snubs the ILO.

ICFTU online (December 4, 1996).

Brussels, December 4, 1996 (ICFTU online): According to information obtained by the ICFTU, the World Trade Organization has withdrawn an invitation for Michel Hansenne, director general of the UN's International Labor Office (ILO), who was expected to participate in the WTO's first-ever Ministerial Conference to take place in Singapore on December 9–13.

"The WTO's refusal to allow the ILO to contribute to its debates bodes ill for the hopes expressed by those who expect the Singapore meeting to voice a minimum of concern and respect for basic workers' rights and living conditions as one of the main objectives behind the international trade agenda," says the ICFTU.

The question of linking trade and respect for basic labor standards is expected to be a major controversy at the WTO conference as governments from Europe, Africa, Latin America, and the United States will table a proposal to establish a WTO working group on the issue and to have the question anchored in the WTO future work program.

ICFTU Is the International Confederation of Trade Unions

According to the ICFTU, the withdrawal of an invitation to ILO's Michel Hansenne, who had originally received an invitation, is part of an offensive launched by a number of governments in the Asia and Pacific region to kill any attempts to discussing workers' rights in the WTO forum.

Asian and Pacific governments have argued that discussions on workers' rights belong to the ILO only and not the WTO, and are fiercely opposed to any linkage between trade and labor standards.

"Discussions on workers' rights belong to the ILO only." Now that's a good one. The ILO are free to discuss their concerns among themselves. How laughable is that?

Yet, notes the ICFTU, the same governments have blocked any progress aimed at strengthening the ILO's capacity to promote these rights. At the ILO Governing Body meeting this November, with the support of the employers' group, they managed to block any progress on the question of strengthening the ILO's means of action for a more effective enforcement of international labor standards and proposed steps, which would result in the undermining of the ILO's existing procedures and supervisory mechanisms.

If you think US workers have had a tough time of economic justice, read on.

All evidence points to the fact that governments and their agents are interested in products, not people. All the international organizations we have mentioned, or will yet mention, in *Imperfect Partners* possess anti-labor sentiments. Truly they intend to band the corporations together with express global freedoms to make trade easier and more profitable, at the same time that they segregate labor and force them to remain scattered, isolated, and jurisdictional, otherwise minimizing solidarity and influence.

Asian and Pacific governments: "A number of these governments pay scant regard to their workers' rights and conditions and while maneuvering to avoid discussion in Singapore in the name of ostensibly strengthening the ILO, International Labor Organization, they spare no efforts to weaken the UN's only tripartite agency."

The ICFTU, International Confederation of -Trade Unions.

The ICFTU, which groups trade union centers from both developing and industrialized countries, has been campaigning for the opening of markets through liberalization of tariffs to be linked to respect of seven basic ILO conventions, including the ban on child and forced labor, the freedom of workers to form trade unions and bargain conditions with their employers, and non-discrimination in employment.

It will organize a major international trade union conference in Singapore on the eve of the WTO event, and a number of trade unionists will attend the WTO conference to lobby government delegations.

"The barring of the ILO from attending such an important event whose results will affect workers worldwide flies in the face of freedom of expression and democratic dialogue, which govern the system of universal concentration as normally applied by the UN and related inter-governmental organizations," the ICFTU concluded.

For details, contact ICFTU Press at ++322 224 02 12. Other online news on Poptel Bulletin Board ICFTU-Online for Geonet users and on the WWW at http://www.icftu.org.

It really doesn't matter to the lawmakers as to how many labor organizations exist, so long as they are relatively powerless. When the WTO can de-invite an organization such as the ILO, an agency within the UN, without so much as a statement of contest from the UN, it is easy to see who is in the driver's seat.

Read it again.

Part of an offensive launched by a number of governments in the Asia and Pacific region to kill any attempts to discussing workers' rights in the WTO forum.

The boldness to label such anti-labor sentiments as "an offensive launched" about says it all and leaves nothing unsaid or hidden about how governments in general really feel about the well-being of their own citizenry in our-ever expanding global economy. It is not just about what we see and hear concerning physical crackdowns and belligerent worker abuses in places like China. In the United States of America, we are too sophisticated to lash out so crudely.

In the USA, the only evidence left to evaluate how anti-labor our governing body is, is to see and understand the process implemented to change working Americans from economic ability to economic disability. That has been made easy simply by removing "Made in America" to places more economically deprived and more easily manipulated. Oh, and with the assistance of our sitting Congresses.

Ideological free-market absolutism has about identical earmarks with what I call corporate communism. While we have political representation in, Washington it is easily apparent that they are mostly window dressing or dispatch carriers for those who are really in charge: corporate bosses.

When you get down to who exerts domination in global economics, the corporations are clearly in the driver's seat. Furthermore, I have pointed out that the created agencies— WTO, IMF, UN, etc.—are nothing more than tools for the multinational corporations to use to implement their agenda to control the new global economy and usher in the new world order.

How Big Is the ICFTU?

Claiming 157 million members in 225 affiliated organizations in 148 countries and territories, the International Confederation of Free Trade Unions (ICFTU) came into being on December 7, 1949. The ICFTU has three regional organizations. Central to the ICFTU's work has been the struggle to defend workers' rights.

As big as the ICFTU is, it is of little importance and powerless without support in the lawmaking bodies. That is where the power lies to change the way the world does business. I have suggested in theory that if the workers of the world were able to organize in one cohesive union and embrace solidarity, then and only then could workers level the economic playing field on a global scale and bring economic stability into the global arena.

I have to state the following as a question for the experts and economists to give opinion on, as I am an ordinary citizen and do not know the answer to the following:

By organizing strong global worker unionization, contributing to a level economic playing field, this, in turn, would smooth out the ridiculously wide mountain and valley swing effects to stock markets, currency fluctuations, interest rates, etc., etc. Real estate values would resemble actual value versus hyper-inflated or false values.

The lists can go on and on, but to put this economic model of global unionization of workers in a nutshell, is to replace our present global economic senselessness with common sense that fulfills the tenets of what defines an economy with ethical, moral, and social values.

From www. Investor words.com

Economy: Activities related to the production and distribution of goods and services in a particular geographic region. The correct and effective use of available resources.

While many of us may have regarded the correct and effective use of available resources as inconsequential, immaterial, and irrelevant in the beginning of *Imperfect Partners*, now that we have accumulated data to paint a much-bigger picture of the global economy and how the corporations and their political partners are working the system that they created, there is a desperate need to create a counter system or to affect a market correction—like that of a stock market correction—to bring checks and balance to their senseless economic assault that best defines war on the middle class at the least, and political and economic terrorism at most.

There Is No Such Thing as an Unskilled Person

Most of us have likely joined in laughter about how much money could be made if domestic engineer (homemakers) were paid what they are actually worth. That is, mothers/fathers/companions, nannies etc., who opt to stay home and cook, clean, care for children, do errands, shopping, banking and those who do it for a living.

When you take a closer look at the skill required to effectively carry out those domestic duties, with the frugality of an economist and the precision of a craftsman, you can see it is no longer a laughing matter but rather a real necessity and hard work that cannot be left undone.

Unfortunately, keeping the fire burning at home is being left undone, and the result is exactly what you can expect. What we are seeing all across America is the ever increase in forms of hooliganism, gangs, illicit drug epidemics, split families, crime waves, escalating poverty, etc., etc.

Between the 1970s and the 1990s

It is the ultra rich who are casting the aura of minimal value for doing work that requires less than a college degree, and now that more workers than ever before in history have variations of advanced education, they (corporations) are beginning to seek skilled workers from low-income societies to replace skilled American workers. Only since skilled American workers, most holding a sheepskin and having become a target have they become concerned for their own safety from becoming a casualty of the "war on the middle class."

A Congressman was once asked if he could define pornography. Giving thought to the question momentarily, he said, "No, but I know it when I see it."

What do we the people *see* to explain how our American corporations can be mostly credited for de-capitalizing American workers? Here are just five elements that, without doubt, have contributed greatly to the multinational corporations' domination for global economic exploitation.

Firstly, American corporations dried up America's manufacturing base to take advantage of low-cost labor and easy access in third-world struggling nations. Secondly, they paid for play with American politics. Thirdly, they brainchild bogus trade deals, like NAFTA, and American politicians from both Democratic and Republican administrations swallowed the hook on corporate tutelage of creating thousands of high-paying jobs and expanded prosperity for all. This was simply an outright fabrication.

Fourthly, despotic rogue leaders in poverty-stricken nations are known to sell out their own people for self-enrichment. Fifthly, they infiltrated or commandeered organizations like the WTO, UN, IMF, and World Bank to promote an agenda of policies making trade easier and circumvent national sovereignty laws.

Over time, the evidence has mounted up so conclusively that it is difficult to deny that corporate America had bought and paid for a partnership with the political establishment. Industries and their spear-carriers, economic ladder have been so proficient at insulating themselves, utilizing power and position to create their own rules for each other. For example, a CEO will enact loan forgiveness to an assistant or junior executive who sits on the board and who, in turn, votes for increases or bonuses for the CEO. They, in effect, take good care of each other, and we the people seem powerless to change this behavior.

It has been reported that in Japanese society, a CEO would be ashamed to take more than $250,000 in compensation for his job and what value he can contribute to the business. Apparently in America we do not share this kind of humility.

Different Strokes for Different Folks

As of July 24, 2008, the federal minimum-wage law stands at $6.55 per hour and not having a raise since 1997. Comparing this status to US Congressmen: at the time of the 1963 march on Washington, members of Congress earned *nine times* the pay of minimum-wage workers. Now, they earn *fifteen times* as much.

The point is not how much more they earn; the point is how much their pay has gone up to remain comfortable for the times in which we live. Please remember, salaries are only a small portion of wealth accessible to our hardworking congressional representatives. Lobbyists are padding their accounts in a way that probably makes their salaries look like a middle-school student's lunch money.

There would not be twelve million Mexicans and tens of thousands from Central and South America risking their lives to trek long dangerous miles to scale a fence that is projected to cost up to thirty-four billion to enter the USA illegally, and we would not be spending more billions of dollars in manpower to repel illegal immigration, if we designed our economic system for prosperity rather than poverty, and by recognizing the true value of labor. Remember, if Mexicans could make what they should in Mexico, they would cease to come and we would have to offer incentives for immigrants.

We the people are becoming all too aware of what the priority has been for far too long. Reform is the political in word. Little by little, they are testing the waters to see if the American people will accept their idea of reforms. Don't be sucked in until their plan for reform is clearly defined line by line. Reform may sound like "just what the doctor ordered." Don't be too quick to nod for their prescription; the side effects could bring on an unbearable headache.

It has been very quiet on the issue of social security reforms as of 2008. It is too early to tell what will transpire under the incoming administration; therefore, the working class had better be prepared if or when reforming our social programs comes to the forefront.

I wrote the following paragraph at least a year or two before Barack Obama ran for and was elected as our forty-fourth president. As you can see, I began writing *Imperfect Partners* several years ago.

What we need far more than reform is new blood representing a new culture, envisioning a new direction for America.

It's Easy to Say It but Difficult to See It

There is a major problem with implementing a new direction. Depending on which political party is out of power, a new direction to them amounts to only that ten cents' worth of difference between each party if they can unseat the incumbents. You may say we have changed direction since the beginning of time. The more we change, the more our direction remains the same.

If anyone was to ask for my opinion as to how to implement economic and political change that would amount to truly a new direction, I would chime in with some of those congressmen or congresswomen who famously said, "Where is Ross Perot when you need him?" Mr. Perot was emphatic about putting America first. My estimation is that he was a leader ahead of his time.

America was used to the old establishment under Republican and Democratic administrations, and middle America was not yet pushed to the economic breaking point.

Going Back to the 1950s

Just when the American dream was becoming a reality for workers under labor leaders like Walter Reuther and Jimmy Hoffa, American infrastructure was making America a formidable contender economically, militarily, and politically—corporate America was readying to take the game from local to international.

Just a few short years out of WW II and rebuilding Japan from ashes, the squeeze on our powerful unions would begin almost without notice. Corporate America was readying to take their game to new playgrounds. Japan would be the first in a chain of opportunities yet to be discovered by corporate America.

Between do-nothing Congresses and the courts, all the gains and aspirations for millions of workers living the American dream would become closer to the American nightmare.

Thirty Years Later

As of January 2009, Congress is debating the passage of the Employee Free Choice Act. I suspect that this act is in response to make labor feel good about an incoming Democratic administration, whose platform purports more support for working Americans, as opposed the traditional Republican Party's philosophy of trickle-down economics.

President-elect Obama has said he wants to bring back the middle class. Bill Clinton was a Democrat also, and as you have read, his record with NAFTA (1994) and giving China most-favored-nation status has contributed more to the loss of the middle class than ever before in history.

Following forty years under both Republican and Democratic administrations, even strong unions have been made ineffective with globalization. And now that Obama is taking the helm, for him to think of pushing the Employee Free Choice Act is an avenue to help bring back the middle class. This is not an avenue but rather a dirt road leading to a dead end. Regardless of what either political party purports to say about how they support workers, their results speak for themselves.

In the Beginning of His Term, Clinton Was Against MFN Status for China

"Alarmed by Clinton's original insistence on linking trade to human rights, corporate lobbyists launched a massive campaign in 1994 which succeeded in reversing Clinton's position."

"The result," observed the *New York Times*, "has been an extraordinary struggle pitting executives against former torture victims and prison-camp survivors and persecuted Christians in a competition to win the attention of Congress and the administration."

"In the final weeks leading up to Clinton's decision to grant most-favored-nation trading status to China, Washington was swarming with lobbyists pushing MFN," stated the *Legal Times*. "The advocates ranged from an Ad hoc group of two dozen major US companies to the Emergency Committee for American Trade (ECAT), a group of 60 chairmen and chief executives of US-owned exporters... Among the lobbyists taking part were R. D. Folsom, a vice president at the D.C. lobby shop R. Duffy Wall and Associates, who represents the Footwear Distributors and Retailers of America; Michael Daniels, a partner in the D.C. office of the New York law firm Mudge Rose Guthrie Alexander & Ferdon; and Mark McConnell and Warren Maruyama, partners at the D.C. law firm Hogan & Hartson."

As a face-saving measure, Clinton drafted a "voluntary code of conduct" for US businesses operating in China and other countries where human rights violations occur. The "voluntary code" came under immediate criticism from Amnesty International and other human-rights organizations.

"It's essentially milquetoast; it lacks political will," said Jim O'Dea, Amnesty International's Washington director.

Source: http://www.sourcewatch.org/index.php?title=Mandarins_and_Moguls_Unite_for_China's_Most-Favored_Nation_Status

"Voluntary code of conduct." Someone must believe we the people are really stupid.

Clinton certainly had his ethics and moral values readjusted.

By the way, do you still think China is our greatest trade competitor? Early on, China was enjoying the millions of jobs being cast their way by American investment. The only competition at that time was American workers competing against Chinese slave labor producing products in China for the American consumer.

In reality there was no competition. It was only a case of American corporations enjoying enhanced means of production, distribution, and sales revenue. As time moved on, China would prove to learn a lot from the American corporations; So much so that they set up their own enterprises that finally you could say China is now a real competitor.

Congress should have seen this coming and done their job in countering, but they must have thought this was so big that it would never rear up to bite them. Even today, you will not hear anyone pointing the finger of blame for such incompetent leadership. They will always point to China as the culprit for causing our tremendous indebtedness and trade imbalance.

It isn't China's fault, folks. Our leadership laid the pathway for China to take advantage of an opportunity.

Is it getting easier to see why I have labeled this whole fiasco perpetrated by our highest leadership as economic and political terrorism? And not a shot was fired.

As you can easily see, Clinton bowed like a willow branch in the wind when big money began to speak. The point is this: unions have historically fared no better under Democratic administrations than they did under Republican administrations. When those we elect are faced with a choice of whom to serve versus to whom they are indebted, the choice is clear.

The Employee Free Choice Act is nothing more than smoke and mirrors to make the working men and women of the USA believe that Congress and the White House are working overtime to restore what some mysterious someone else, from some mysterious other place has caused us to lose economic footing, and this act is going to empower workers to stand up to their employers and bargain, thus restoring at least some of our great economic losses. Not only do I believe it will not work, it may even be counterproductive for the American worker. What do you think?

My summary of the Employee Free Choice Act: even if forming unions is made easier, they will be mostly ineffective because of corporate threat and mobility to lock out, shut down, and move on. Washington knows this—and so should everyone else.

We have previously reviewed the vastness of corporate multinational holdings that most corporations have (e.g., Carrier Corp., a subsidiary of United Technologies). With corporate America having such vast capabilities to shift production and distribution to anywhere on earth, they have little need to negotiate anything, anywhere, or anytime.

I personally believe the Employee Free Choice Act has amounted to little more than a political football to get needed votes from desperate workers with false hope. It creates an illusion that they are working hard for a good cause. Promoting worker empowerment will go a long way toward getting votes when, in reality, they are forging meaningless measures that accomplish more status quo. This bill was first introduced in both chambers of Congress on March 10, 2009.

"It's Baaack! The Employee Free Choice Act's Arbitration Requirement for an Initial Collective Bargaining Agreement Is New and Not So Improved."

Info from Barran Liebman.com.

On January 4, 2013, Rep. Gene Green (D-TX) proposed a bill known as the Labor Relations First Contract Act (LRFCA, HR. 169). Oh well, I guess they needed a new face on an old character.

I do realize that the AFL-CIO leaders are staunchly advocating this act, and I realize why they would be. Aside from filling important union officers' positions, the AFL-CIO is a dedicated worker-advocacy organization. Membership drives have been initiated before, and it never stopped corporate America from snubbing them with the threat of relocating to foreign locations that they already own or have a stake in. Along with this threat, any local labor union belonging to the AFL-CIO was left to negotiate the concessions offered just to retain jobs and fend off more lost benefits and wage concessions.

All this anarchy exists simply because our sitting Congresses of the past, present, and probably future—Democratic or Republican administrations—have done exactly as Tom Teppen said: "Industries and their spear-carriers, among political conservatives are working together to make sure that the U.S. government will (fail) to take any actions that could inconvenience the industries or offend conservatives ideological free market absolutism."

(Quotes by Tom Teepen, Cox News Service, under the title "The menace of political degeneracy").

Obviously, Teepen is a liberal, but he is right. However, if a conservative made the same determination, it is doubtful that there would be little disagreement.

As I have previously said, I believe that the global economy has become far too pervasive in every aspect of the lives of world citizens. To think you can manage it in a jurisdictional sense by establishing such things as the Employee Free Choice Act for American workers amounts to too little, too late, or a day late and a dollar short.

The fact remains that it is and has always been the responsibility of Congress to manage international trade looking out for American interests, and they have totally disregarded that primary responsibility, period.

The Employee Free Choice Act, even its name emanates a split down the middle to divide rather than unite, or the new version, the First Contract Act (LRFCA, HR. 169) makes about as much half hearted challenges as handing a person a round-point shovel and telling him/her to start shoveling to fill in the Mississippi river and change its course.

The Labor Movement Has Been through This Before; Closed Shop and Right-to-Work Law Is Nothing New

For a period after the passage of the Wagner Act (see National Labor Relations Board) in 1935, decisions of the federal courts tended to uphold the legality of the closed shop, which required employees to be a union member. Many states, however, either by legislation or by court decision, have banned the closed shop.

In 1947, the Taft-Hartley Labor Act declared the closed shop illegal, and union shops were also prohibited unless authorized in a secret poll by a majority of the workers; it was amended (1951) to allow union shops without a vote of the majority of the workers. Thereafter, a campaign was begun by business leaders in certain industries to have so-called right-to-work laws enacted at the state level.

More than one-third of the states passed such laws, the effect being to declare the union shop illegal. It is argued in favor of the closed shop that unions can win a fair return for their labor only through solidarity, since there is always— except in wartime—an oversupply of labor, and that, since all employees of a plant share in the advantages won through collective bargaining, all workers should contribute to union funds.

Arguments in favor of the open shop are that forcing unwilling workers to pay union dues is an infringement of their rights.

Let's keep our focus on the root of the problem. Our biggest problem is not about whether to be pro union or non union. The real problem facing American workers is at the Washington-level leadership failure to take any actions that could inconvenience the industries or offend ideological free-market absolutism.

After forty years of this kind of inaction, their new action is to try to sweep past actions under the rug with more of the same but give it a new name. The new name or the new game that absolves them of incompetence to lead and protect is to blame it on the new global economy. That was easy.

US district judge Ricardo M. Urbina refused the request from the United Farm Workers and Farmworker Justice to stop the Labor Department from instituting new H2-A visa rules.

Actually, the Department of Labor is so ineffective in establishing unbiased equality that it would be best to eliminate this agency and start from scratch. They are so politically motivated and entrenched that reforming it would be akin to attempting to build a skyscraper on a foundation of sand.

Simply review the history of the minimum-wage law—immigrant workers agriculture, in particular, HB-2 (revised)—to get a pretty vivid picture of what this agency has actually accomplished for the American people in particular since its inception (1913).

Let's remember that temporary (immigrant) status has been changed from ten months to three years, and on top of that, corporations have stepped up the game from unskilled to skilled, including professionals such as scientists, etc. Is it any wonder why the sociologists at our top universities have modified their view toward the workforce in general, now that they have a pony in the show?

When we examine the history of the organizations designed to look out for worker's interests, we see it paints a pretty dismal picture. Actually, there is literally no governmental agency that is attempting to support worker rights, working conditions, and improving pay; unless you are looking for ways to meet the minimum or get to a lower standard through reform.

What would it take to upgrade the plight of not only war on the middle class in the USA but also, as we have reviewed, denial by the WTO and the UN to give the ILO a seat in meetings? I really don't have a problem of affixing a new label on such actions as economic and political terrorism.

Are you beginning to see the disdain all politically inspired humanitarian agencies really have for workers of the new global economy? Governments by and large appear to be totally controlled by elitists. Follow the money, and you will know who rules the world.

While we do not condone slavery, beatings, inequality, or unfair practices anymore, the question is, what is it that we do condone?

It is easy to see the flippant dedication and wet gunpowder of the United Nations when a working people's agency such as the ILO can be denied participation in the WTO. And the UN doesn't even respond. What a powerhouse! Again, I have said, if you believe that global agencies like the WTO, UN, and others that act as overseeing institutions on humanitarian issues are looking out for workers' issues and rights equally in the new world order, I urge you to take a second look.

The federal minimum-wage law has been on the books since 1938, and it is like having a 1959 American Motors Rambler for your primary means of transportation. They are so behind the times and ineffective that many employers already pay employees more than the minimum wage law requires. That is all the more reason to do something drastic with the agency.

Will We Solve Our Health Care Crisis?

Dennis Kucinich, Democratic congressman from Ohio, in his bid as a presidential candidate in 2008.

"Some want to make it mandatory for people to have health insurance, but what they are not mandating is the money insurance companies can make. People can have health insurance, but be in worse shape after treatment with the deductibles, co-pays, and premiums," he said. "It should be a basic right in a democratic society, not a privilege based on your ability to pay."

Our health care industry is not exportable. It is generally unaffordable, and because it is a necessity, it is not the same as buying a less-expensive automobile because it is all you can afford. The less-expensive auto will get you to where you need to go, but buying health care that you may only be able to afford may not restore an unhealthy condition, and may even cost you your life.

We are going to revisit several events that could rightly be labeled social eras. We all are familiar with Martin Luther King's crusade, "I Have a Dream" message that most Americans equate with black versus white.

The one element of his movement that seems to have escaped us is his call for economic justice. Most of us hardly even give economic justice a glancing thought when we hear "I have a dream" over and over. We only think in terms of black versus white. Mr. King was also talking about parity for all people.

Walter Reuther stood by King's side when he gave that speech in 1963. There were a few in King's time who connected to his vision. Unfortunately, black and white could not establish solidarity in that time. Had that been possible, America may have economically advanced forty years ahead of where we are now. Let me say that again to make it perfectly understood: if black and white could have put aside their color differences and united under economic-equality issues, could the world have become a different place?

Do All Terrorists Wear Combat Boots and Carry Backpacks Filled with Explosives?

The stagnation of King's dream effort most likely was caused by political and racial adversity that directly stunted the economic, social, and cultural progress of our nation as a whole.

What is the underlying theme of the adversity that I am implying? It goes like this: I will do nothing to hurt you, neither will I do anything to help you.

Likewise, the stagnation of American workers getting any action from Washington to do their job in managing America's well-being in the global economy, without doubt, has been driven by the top 2 percent of the world's population, more commonly recognized as the elite. And what influence do they wield? "Industries and their spear-carriers, are working together to make sure that the US government will fail to take any actions that could inconvenience the industries or offend ideological free market absolutism."

Democrats and Republicans alike have proven by their very actions to do everything possible not to inconvenience the industries or offend free-market absolutism. Following forty years of inept leadership, we can conclusively determine that congressional (partnering) with big business successfully collapsed the economy of the USA. Hence, fulfilling one of the important tenants of why I labeled this book *Imperfect Partners*.

If There Is One Thing This World Needs, It Is Understanding

Ralph C. Smedley, the single founder of the world-renowned public-speaking international organization Toastmasters, said, "If there is one thing this world needs, it is understanding."

Possibly what this world needs today, more than anything else, is leadership that understands what we the people already understand. We the working people have a dream! It doesn't take a lot of study to determine that our politicians don't share our vision, nor do they come close to a "United we stand, divided we fall" philosophy.

Imperfect Partners is designed around a broad spectrum of imperfect high-level leadership that have missed the mark of equality and justice for all. The focus and aims of this writer's intent is to recognize Americans as a whole, and many middle-class workers in particular, for unequal representation cast by those whom we the people voted in office to uphold their duty to protect the interests of all equally. This book covers condensed diverse subject matter that would otherwise require several books to accomplish the same end.

The rich heritage of our country can be attributed to the fearless courage of some of the most "unlikely to succeed." The great companies of America almost exclusively began with one person with a dream.

America is known as the melting pot. A diversity of immigrant and native-born individuals who contributed mightily to our nation and mankind. Many never gained recognition due them until well beyond their own death. We will be recognizing some of them. To begin, here is the first of several interesting founders of the American dream come true.

Andrew Carnegie

Tough early beginnings and lessons learned about the power of knowledge from a local merchant with a library made Andrew Carnegie not only one of the world's richest men but also one of its most giving.

Born to working-class parents, Margaret and Will Carnegie, on November 25, 1835, in Dunfermline, Scotland. When Carnegie died in Lenox, Massachusetts, on August 11, 1919, his steel empire had produced the raw materials that built the infrastructure of the United States. More importantly, he had given away more than $350 million and had founded the development of over three thousand libraries worldwide.

The son of a skilled weaver, Carnegie grew up in a working-class family and was expected to take up the weaving trade. The coming of the industrialist age and automated weaving looms changed those expectations, however, and when the Carnegie family immigrated to the United States in 1848, they were penniless.

Carnegie's father was greatly discouraged by his inability to support his family, and his mother made it clear that she was greatly disappointed in her husband and saddened by their poverty. Well-aware of the difficulty of the situation, and pushed by his mother's determination to see him succeed, Carnegie took a job working as a bobbin boy in a loom factory for $1.20 a week. His next job as a steam engine and boiler attendant paid $2 a week, but it was his penmanship that impressed his bosses, and he was soon promoted to clerk.

Building on that success, Carnegie took a position as a telegraph boy delivering messages. His rare ability to understand dash-and-dot messages by ear led to his recruitment in 1853 by Thomas Scott, president of the Pennsylvania Railroad. Carnegie proceeded to learn everything he could about the railroad industry while working as Scott's personal secretary and earning $35 a month.

Carnegie's father, however, was not so fortunate. Unable to find work as a weaver, he tried to produce his own materials for sale but found few buyers. He died in 1855 when Andrew was only twenty.

The younger Carnegie continued to gain more stature at the Pennsylvania Railroad, breaking a strike before it developed by passing on the names of the strike organizers to his boss, who fired the organizers immediately. Carnegie also made his first investment at the time, putting $217.50 into the Woodruff Sleeping Car Company. Two years he began receiving a return of about $5,000 per year on his investment.

When Scott was appointed assistant secretary of war during the Civil War, Carnegie went to work in Washington as Scott's right-hand man, helping to organize the military telegraph system. Following the war, Carnegie succeeded Scott as superintendent at the Pennsylvania Railroad. Using his investment money and his increased salary, Carnegie was able to move his mother to an upscale neighborhood, which greatly pleased her.

Carnegie continued to invest in small iron mills and other related companies, which now included the Adams Express Company, the Piper and Schiffler Company, the Central Transportation Company, and an oil company in Titusville, Pennsylvania. By 1863, half of his $42,000 income was derived from investments.

Carnegie retired from the railroad in 1865 and proceeded to concentrate on building his fortune. He reorganized the Piper and Schiffler Company into the Keystone Bridge Company to build bridges from iron rather than wood. He also founded the Keystone Telegraph Company, which was allowed to string telegraph wire on the railroad poles across the entire state. Keystone attracted immediate interest from the Pacific and Atlantic Telegraph Company, allowing its investors to triple their return.

Carnegie's investment income was almost $50,000 per year by 1868, and although he'd promised himself he'd retire from business and devote himself to philanthropy and education at the age of thirty-five, a trip to England resulted in a change of plans. After visiting Henry Bessemer's steel plants, whose steel-making process Carnegie he had been using since 1861 at the Freedom Iron Company, he saw great potential to expand the steel business in North America.

Along with several partners, including Henry Frick, Carnegie opened the first steel plant in 1875. The Edgar Thomson Works in Braddock, Pennsylvania, received its first order for two thousand steel rails from Carnegie's former employer, the Pennsylvania Railroad. Carnegie further expanded is empire by purchasing rival steel mill Homestead Works in 1883.

It was around this time that Carnegie began to publish some serious written works on social and political issues, including *Round the World* (1881), *An American Four-in-Hand in Britain* (1883), and *Triumphant Democracy* (1886). The latter publication celebrated the American belief in democracy and capitalism and compared America's social system with that of many unequal European class-based systems. It also praised the American educational system. Additionally, Carnegie supported unions with an article in Forum Magazine defending workers' rights.

Tragedy also struck the Carnegie family in 1886. Carnegie himself became very sick with typhoid, and both his mother and brother died. Heart struck by the death of his family, Carnegie married his longtime girlfriend Louise Whitfield.

This sequence of events surely had a profound effect on Carnegie's feelings about life and work, and led him to write his most famous manuscript, "The Gospel of Wealth," in 1889. Published in the 1889 *North American* review, the article argued that the rich should use their wealth to benefit their communities as a whole. In the article, Carnegie said, "a man who dies rich dies disgraced."

Andrew Carnegie had one child, a daughter, Margaret Carnegie, in 1897, after which the Carnegie family purchased Skibo Castle in Scotland. Carnegie decided he needed to spend more time on research and development and subsequently moved to New York. He also spent six months of the year in Scotland with his family.

In 1889 Carnegie made Henry Frick chairman of the Carnegie Company, a mistake he would later regret. While in Scotland in 1892, Frick decided to reduce piecework rates for the steel workers, which led to the infamous Homestead Strike by the Amalgamated Iron and Steel Workers Union at

Carnegie's Homestead plant. Frick hired three hundred strike breakers, but when they got to the plant, the strikers were waiting for them.

In a daylong battle, ten men were killed and sixty wounded before the governor placed Homestead under martial law. Carnegie took responsibility for the deaths but was greatly discouraged by Frick's actions and saddened by the fact that his name would never again be associated with supporting the working man.

Despite the tragedy, the Carnegie Steel Company continued to expand over the next ten years. By 1899, annual production of steel was 2,663,412 tons with profits of $40 million. Conflicts between Carnegie and Henry Frick were also finally resolved in 1899, when Carnegie bought out Frick for $15 million.

Two years later, Frick and J. P. Morgan purchased the Carnegie Steel Company for $500 million and renamed it the US Steel Corporation. The new company was valued at $1.4 billion, and left Carnegie with a personal fortune of $225 million.

After the sale of his company, Carnegie began to concentrate more seriously on philanthropy.

He had already established the Carnegie Institute of Pittsburgh (1895). And eleven years prior to the sale of his company, he had offered the city of Pittsburgh $1 million to build the Carnegie Library of Pittsburgh. Carnegie's love of reading developed from his childhood experience in the library of a local businessman, and he had always wanted to make the reading experience available to everyone as a means of self-education. But he had more to do.

In 1902, he founded the Carnegie Institution of Washington to provide research for American colleges and universities. In 1905, he established the Carnegie Teachers' Pension Fund with an endowment of $10 million, and also the Carnegie Institute of Technology. In 1910, he established the Carnegie Endowment for International Peace.

In 1911, the Carnegie Corporation was established with approximately $125 million, its goal being to aid colleges, universities, technical schools, and scientific research. In 1913, the Carnegie United Kingdom Trust was established, followed in 1914 by the Carnegie Council on Ethics and International Affairs.

Carnegie returned home to Scotland for one last time at the outbreak of the war in 1914. In 1916, he bought Shadowbrook, an estate in Lenox, Massachusetts, where he would live for the remainder of his life.

When he died in 1919, his gravestone read simply, "Andrew Carnegie, Born in Dunfermline, Scotland, 25 November 1835. Died in Lenox, Massachusetts, 11 August 1919."

His proudest words remain forever carved in stone above the Carnegie Library of Pittsburgh: "Free to the People."

For more information about the Carnegie Corporation, please visit http://www.carnegie.org/.

For more information about Andrew Carnegie, please visit http://www.pbs.org/wgbh/amex/carnegie/.

It is reported that he regretted his involvement with Henry Frick, who invariably could be said to have the blood of ten men on his hands. However, Carnegie took full responsibility for that action. Carnegie went from ratting on strikers to supporting unions and workers' rights.

Carnegie began to publish some serious written works on social and political issues, including *Round the World* (1881), *An American Four-in-Hand in Britain* (1883), and *Triumphant Democracy* (1886). The latter publication celebrated the American belief in democracy and capitalism, and compared America's social system with that of many unequal European class-based systems.

Carnegie was all too familiar with "unequal European class-based systems." As having lived under its cruel hand, just as those of us reading *Imperfect Partners* who have had our heads on the economic chopping block can identify with what is surely but not so slowly becoming a two-class system more closely aligned to what Carnegie came to despise.

The principle of trickle-down economics possessed few flaws for the first one hundred years of economic creation and growth in America. Life was much harsher, and society in general was crude and rudimentary, simplistic as the Wild West, where the gun ruled.

We were a society of experimental ideals that relied on learning technical and social sophistication. There is one thing that industrialization seems to bring about: social sophistication. Hard labor in the steel mills, etc., along with slow but rising wages meant a better life, as workers for the first time began to spend their hard-earned money for activities of social and cultural enlightenment. You might say the American workforce was becoming more sophisticated and saw the American dream as an attainable goal.

The days when sophisticated people naturally ruled over less-sophisticated people with an iron fist would be mellowing out. Unionization of workers was growing in those early days. The life of Riley was coming into its own.

George Eastman

George Eastman, the founder of the Eastman Kodak Company, was one of the few mavericks of his time. By any economic standard, he was unorthodox.

Eastman did not believe in paying his workers as little as possible. He believed that by sharing the wealth of the company it would propel the company into one of the great companies of the world, a principle that proved itself by what it produced.

Kodak employees have never had a Union workforce, as there never was the need for it. We must remember that unions were formed in most cases for one reason: there was a need for them. Eastman maintained a different approach in labor relations. In my words, and as I excerpted earlier in this book, "he made a place where others could do it."

Rochester, New York, has several cultural landmarks in the Rochester area that still stand as a testament to the high principles of Eastman's business leadership, and the area is one of the most prosperous in central New York State that can be attributed to his legacy.

Unfortunately, there are not very many George Eastmans around, and the only other way to get economic equality has been by utilizing the bargaining system.

We can appreciate the benefit of hindsight. We have just completed reviewing a condensed synopsis of the legacy of Andrew Carnegie. His mark on history can be seen, felt, and experienced to this day. While he seemingly lacked the compassion of George Eastman, he was a grassroots player, who could claim to know what it was like to roll up his sleeves and make his dream come true.

There is a point to be seen and felt through reviewing the history of our people, places, and events, and it is this: by specific examples, we can relate to the principle of cause and effect. Lest we forget, the tremendous contributions of entrepreneurs like Carnegie and Eastman are still working today, impacting us socially, culturally, and economically.

It has been said, "To understand where we are going, we need to understand our past and our present."

For instance, if we visit Rochester, New York, we could visit the Eastman house, gardens, library, archives and study center, school of music, etc. In the midst of Eastman's endless legacy, we would discover just how passionately he demonstrated his sincerity for cultural and educational progress, equally important with economics.

If you were to get a guided tour of the Eastman Theater, you would be pleasantly surprised to discover all seats are the same price. Only a very few were reserved for special guests. Eastman believed that every person who wanted to experience the cultural benefits of music should have the opportunity.

When we say "Make a difference" or "Make a place where others can do it," we have the example of those who have a proven record: meet Dr. Ralph C. Smedley, the founder of Toastmasters International.

Dr. Ralph C. Smedley 1

"The unprepared speaker has a right to be afraid" (Dr. Ralph C. Smedley, 1878–1965).

The story of Ralph Smedley's early work with Toastmasters is a testimony to his insight and tenacity. While working for the YMCA, he discovered that many young men were tongue-tied and awkward in their presentations. To help them improve, he created a club where they could practice public speaking in an atmosphere of acceptance and assistance.

The idea was a success: the young men's skills improved. However, the club was not self-sustaining. Four times, Dr. Smedley was transferred by his employer, and each time, a club he left behind eventually died.

After sixteen years, he was finally transferred to Santa Ana, California, where his concept of self-sustaining clubs for the practice and improvement of public speech grew into reality, establishing a strong-enough foothold to thrive on their own.

Dr. Smedley established Toastmasters as "a nonprofit, noncommercial movement, for the benefit of its members," and never made a penny from his creation. He worked for the YMCA until retirement at the age of sixty-three, and then volunteered his services to Toastmasters until shortly before his death at eighty-seven.

The organization grew out of a single club, Smedley Club Number 1, which would become the first Toastmasters club. It was founded by Ralph C. Smedley on October 22, 1924, at the YMCA in Santa Ana, California.

Toastmasters International was incorporated under California law on December 19, 1932. Throughout its history, Toastmasters has served over four million people, and today, the organization serves over 250,000 members in 108 countries.

Making a Difference

The passion of Eastman and the compassion of Smedley, while from opposite ends of the spectrum, demonstrates trueness in conviction and compassion to their personal cause to "create the place where others can do it."

Where others can do it: Eastman experienced what it was to become prosperous, and he was motivated in creating the environment where every employee of his Kodak Co. could experience a life of shared values in a similar way.

Smedley, on the other hand, had little personal wealth, but what he did have was an unselfish abundance of understanding that the fear of standing before a group of your peers and communicating is more widespread than most people are willing to admit to, and as he said, "I saw a need, and I met it."

These examples illustrate positive results. These are time- and field-tested idealists. You would think that our well-educated world leaders would embrace teaching models, when they see them, as tools to erect political platforms and economic policy that make sense.

You would think they would use the same kind of wisdom that the unidentified Congressman deployed when asked to explain what constituted pornography: "I know it when I see it." Do our leaders possess a slowness to learn from example? Do they believe that because they are elected that they have nothing to learn by listening? Does their record support the reasoning that they are giving we the people a reactionary form of government?

I think the answer to both of these questions is yes. Let's remember, reactionary lacks the element of passion, planning, and willingness for change.

Many, if not most, of our multinational corporations were originally birthed by a single person with a dream. By the time the founder passed their successes on to their children, and then their children's children, we have inherited a generation or two that have never experienced humble beginnings.

The reality is that many of those who are at the helm of today's corporations are those born of inherited fortunes from the self-starters. A portion of them possess ideals of what only a silver-spoon inheritance is able to reproduce. These upper class who are now in charge of extreme wealth with what appears to have left them with a disconnect with anyone outside their own class status.

On the Inside

There was a time in the maturing of our nation when what the boss got paid was less relevant. More than likely not only was he/she the boss, but also they owned the company.

Lock, stock, and barrel. I don't think anyone should argue with this type of ownership.

The Phrase Finder

Originally, I've seen it suggested that this phrase refers to all of a shopkeeper's possessions: the stock in trade, the items stored in barrels, and the lock to the door. That's entirely fanciful, though. The "whole thing" in question when this phrase originated was a musket. Muskets were composed of three parts: lock, stock, and barrel.

I thought you may find the term *lock, stock, and barrel* a little refreshing break from the main study.

It's a New Era

Sophisticated industrial production tooling has advanced, from the use of a ruler to using the micrometer, computer-generated, etc., and far beyond. We have evolved from pouring cast iron in sand molds to highly formulated space-age alloys, composites, etc.

Likewise, inspecting for flaws in how and what is fair-value worker compensation from the CEO to the machinist on the factory floor deserves the scrutiny of the microscope. The world has become a close-tolerance economic environment. The day when the boss who owned the business would be showing up to unlock the door is the exception rather than the rule. This is a new and clearly different social, cultural, and economic era.

The day has arrived in which as one progressive economist has said, "There is no such thing as an unskilled worker." There is no such thing as one size fits all. We are in an era of most everyone either being a specialists or specializing in something.

When it comes to gauging the tolerance of compensations for CEOs, corporate boards, and Wall Streeters, you can be assured that when they are referred to as fat cats by even the powerful, such as the president of the United States, that these people are so disconnected from the rest of society that something has gone awry.

We quite realistically are in a state of economic warfare! Our war is not American workers versus foreign workers; it is American *and* foreign workers being used as cannon fodder by multinational corporations against each other. They are using mobility, power, and political clout to quarantine and reconstitute the global workforce at their pleasure and will to do so.

Everyone enjoys picking on the CEOs, citing their appetite for excess. Does what he/she contribute actually add enough value to the product produced or services marketed to justify the excess they enjoy?

Self-Sufficiency for the Rest of Us)

Our society has set in motion an imaginary or phantom figure that is required as an entry point to be an economic participant.

I have created the phrase "sufficiency for adequate societal integration."

As speculation, I have estimated that $20 per hour would allow a worker to be self-supporting and a contributor. If you can recall, Washington could not even be very specific on what income would be needed to classify middle class.

Instead, corporate management and the Washington 2008 business model, with the recent big two bail out of GM and Chrysler, stipulate that reducing the UAW wages to approximately $14 per hour will make them competitive with non-union foreign manufacturers.

I realize that many people reading *Imperfect Partners* are not going to agree with my hypothesis that "there is no such thing as competition" in much, if not most, of our global economy. A classic example of entanglement is the auto industry. Most Americans know that US auto manufacturers are owners or investors, outsource production and distribution, and share intellectual properties with European and Asian automakers so consistently that it is difficult to tell what make of car you and I are actually driving.

To refer to this business environment as competition is mostly useful for the public relations department as propaganda to reinforce fear and intimidation in the global workforce.

As desperately fearful of deflation as governments are, they sure have a strange way of going about avoiding depreciating the buying power of working Americana. The overall costs of getting things done is just going to have to come down to the new standard somehow. Remember "So goes the big three, so goes the rest of the country"? As the USA continues this downward spiral, and if we do not stop and begin going the other way, what does a total collapse look like?

Charles Everett Koop (October 14, 1916–February 25, 2013) was an American pediatric surgeon and public health administrator. He was a vice admiral in the Public Health Service Commissioned Corps, and served as the thirteenth surgeon general of the United States under President Ronald Reagan from 1982 to 1989. According to the Associated Press, "Koop was the only surgeon general to become a household name."

To underscore the words of Everett Koop, he always banged his head on poverty when he saw any societal problem. "Financial insufficiency for adequate societal integration" are my words to interpret what Koop was saying.

Please read my interpretation again: financial insufficiency for adequate societal integration. If our government continues to sponsor deflating American workers' wages (e.g., UAW), we as a society will be driven more closely to just what they eschew: socialism. How so?

More and more Americans will not have the financial resources to do the very things that corporations and governments want them to do. That is, fund their own retirements, buy their own health care insurance,—last but far from least—pay taxes.

This has been happening for a long time, and as we speak, this is the crisis as to why we no longer can afford to fix our roads and bridges.

Because of the financial ruinous philosophies of world governments in general, it was a timely opportunity for George W. Bush to be in the peculiar position to affect his last successful act to bring labor to its knees.

When Congress could not agree on what to do about the big three, George W. Bush got the chance to earn life kudos from the big two bosses (GM and Chrysler) and all those he plays golf with by attaching governmental conditions to the $14 billion loan that the UAW wages fall into line with the foreign transplant car makers.

Conditions is a pretty close relative to *mandate*, in my book! Of course, this is subject to reversal when Barack Obama is sworn into office on January 20, 2009. This is what the UAW is counting on.

As you read the above paragraph, do you see what I see at work? I see socialism in its highest form. Bailing out corporations with public funding and corporate communism at work simultaneously.

Toyota, Nissan, Honda, Hyundai, and BMW. Yes, they all do have manufacturing facilities in America. For instance, Hyundai has state-of-the-art engineering facilities in Michigan, and design and proving ground facilities in California to boot.

Hyundai in Alabama

"Our $1.1 billion automotive assembly plant is one of the most advanced of its kind. The plant employs more than 2,000 highly skilled workers and began production of the Hyundai Sonata on May 20, 2005, and in 2007 added the Santa Fe to the production line. In 2007, the plant achieved Certification to the International Automotive Task Force's most rigid quality management standard, ISO/TS 16949— the highest automotive operating standard in the world."

Bavarian Motor Works (BMW) has a plant in Spartanburg, South Carolina, that employs over five thousand people. If you visit their website, you will be thoroughly impressed with their technological achievements. For instance, in 2008, they were awarded "World Green Car of the Year." Among some of their innovations is an inline 6 cyl.

clean diesel engine that sips diesel with the efficiency of a 4 cyl. and the power of a V-8. That's impressive engineering.

Hyundai and BMW are the lesser-talked about transplants, yet they sport innovative technology for which the big three apparently need the help of the American taxpayers to finance their engineering advancements to keep them afloat.

The UAW Is Not the Problem

If you are wondering what Detroit has been doing while others have been investing their own money in engineering, listen up. I just finished visiting the Ford Motors website for their Lincoln MKS. And what did I hear in a video portion about this razzle-dazzle creation: engineering actually spent a thousand man hours designing the shift handle for the MKS. They were so proud to announce that!

There are a couple of things I would rather have than a cute shifter. How about a family-size vehicle capable of getting WOW miles per gallon, engineering, or an advanced torsion-bar suspension system that simply needs re-torqueing versus replacing expensive worn-out suspension components?

If this is not feasible, then let the engineers come up with another suspension that does not grow old and lose its resilience to bounce back from potholes we cannot afford to fix. With many of the nation's roads falling into disrepair, we could use a suspension that works as well in old age as when it was new.

How about brake rotors that will never warp or wear thin and need replacement? That would impress most consumers more than a slick shift knob, wouldn't it? I could not believe that Ford, excuse me, *Lincoln* would actually share something like that with the public. And they appear to be in better financial condition than GM and Chrysler.

As far as I can determine, Detroit has proven that the UAW can compete even with reported wages higher than the transplants simply by comparing retail pricing unit for unit.

As I have said, with the riches Detroit had for years, they should be light-years ahead of the Asian or European brands in research and development. Is it as simple as they failed to use their time and wealth to build world-class vehicles but they succeeded in rewarding CEOs and the 1 percent at the top fabulously?

There is not ten cents (price difference) between (comparable) model vehicles produced in Detroit versus any of the transplant non-union companies. When you load either competitor models with equally equipped options, you may even find some non-union produced models actually more expensive than Detroit union labor assembled.

There seems to be widespread acceptance, especially governmental elements that are quick to point the blame finger at the UAW's higher wages as the primary obstacle for

Detroit's inability to compete. I disagree with who is at fault for lagging Detroit.

The only thing UAW workers can control is the quality of their own workmanship on the assembly line. They can only do as good of a job assembling what research and engineering has handed off to them. It all hinges on the engineering of a high-value product, much more than using the excuse of high-cost labor to assemble inferior products.

As US automakers embark on rushing to produce millions of very small vehicles to be put on our freeways, the question is not if they can go fast but can they go fast *safely?* Remember, what Detroit has been talking about is smaller, more-fuel-efficient vehicles. Smaller, more-fuel-efficient just maybe is not what Americans want or need or will buy. How large of a reinforced cage is needed to keep occupants reasonably protected in a severe collision at expressway speeds?

What Do Americans Want Then?

I don't think more research is needed to understand what Americans want in an ideal transportation module. Americans have a longstanding infatuation with the automobile, and they love everything, from small sports cars, trucks, sedans, vans, and vehicles (yet to be engineered).

It's the Cost of Fuel, Stupid!

PS: I am not referring to my readers, I am referring to the saying and the ideology.

It appears that conventional fuel—meaning gasoline—produced from crude oil extracted from the ground has met its limitations. Auto manufacturers are saying they cannot get any more mileage from a gallon of petrol. So they are creating hybrid systems to supplement efforts to stretch a tank full of gas.

I have said that to say this: they have been putting it off for far too long. What they have been putting off is the race to switch fuels being used. They have been partnering with the oil companies beyond the time limit.

2004

Ford and BP have a longstanding cooperation, which aims to develop technology and other solutions to benefit both our "car" and "energy" consumers.

> DETROIT, Oct. 23 /PRNewswire/—BP today dedicated a new hydrogen fueling station as part of a U.S. Department of Energy project designed to facilitate the field-testing of fuel cell vehicles and fuel-

ing infrastructure in the United States.
The program is the next step in bringing hydrogen to broad market distribution. Located at the Next Energy Center
in Detroit, the BP hydrogen station will
supply fuel to DaimlerChrysler fuel cell
vehicles.

I have added these late events by BP and Ford's alliance,
which I believe is a sign of assuring the public of good intentions—good intentions that should have taken place shortly
after the oil embargo of 1974.

I have previously shared with you that the corporate
world will decide when, where, and why they will bring new
products on line.

Why Would They Decide to
Develop New Sources Now?

Fuel sources yet to be developed is of critical importance to addressing our trade deficit. The corporations know
how to gauge the temperature and take the pulse of a nation,
and I believe they realize the temperature of the USA is rising and our pulse is pumping life blood under such pressure
that we are reaching stroke alert. You can be sure they will
release just-enough relief medicine to take our mind off our

many problems while they continue to extract the last drop of profit from available resources.

Eventually, something like hydrogen fuel will be developed and put on line. You can also be assured it will happen at the discretion and pace that the oil companies choose. Again, if what I have said in this paragraph is reality, it also speaks volumes as to who the real world leaders are.

At over $4.00 per gallon for gasoline in mid 2008, will the oil industry be looking for ways to increase domestic production to reduce consumer cost, or will they rely on government subsidization under the guise of research & development?

As I have said, they love capitalism, but when they are on the receiving end, they love socialism.

Henry Ford invented his first car in 1896, but the world-famous Ford Model T was introduced in 1908 with full production by 1912. Mass production is said to have come to maturity by 1927.

So what have American car makers been focusing on since? From the first Model T until around the 1950s, American auto production caused the auto-industry bank accounts to literally burst at the seams.

What to Do with All That Money?

Invest, and invest they did. The car companies had so much money they went looking for places of opportunity, including investing in fossil fuel, gas, and oil. Should we think that there is a connection between the auto industry and the energy industry as to why there is a sluggishness in fuel economy of the automobile?

If you have wondered how those small startup Asian and European car makers came along and knocked the socks off Detroit's big three, here is the reasoning as to how they were able to do it: they learned a lot, and they learned quickly.

They had on their side the ready-made advancements from the American, German, English, etc., to improve upon. You may say they became distracted from their primary purpose. The big three got beaten by their own game, and beaten badly.

I was somewhat encouraged by how president-elect Barack Obama, on December 19, 2008, in a public briefing, said, "I rate our economy by our jobs and wages."

Rate our economy by our jobs and our wages! He has said or implied on various occasions since his election that he is a proponent of unions and decent wages and bringing back the middle class.

You already have an idea of what I think the Employee Free Choice Act will accomplish. Remember, when it gets down to reality, there has never been but ten cents' worth of difference between Democrats and Republicans.

If there ever was a nation that we were disadvantaged to compete with economically, it would be China. Yet Bill gave them the thumbs-up. Why? I would suspect that corporate money can accomplish a lot more in four minutes than American voters can accomplish in four years.

Between concessions and outsourcing, labor will soon be back where they started in the 50s: adjusting for inflation. The same is true of equal opportunity. It has been reported about Martin Luther King, if he could see how little a decent wage for black people has moved (adjusting for inflation) since the 60s, he would roll over in his grave.

Minimum wage is akin to the health care costs crisis, only at opposite poles. The two are predicated for use in an economic environment that does not exist. Minimum wage is absolutely useless, and its rules might as well be shredded to save the office space.

Health care cost are so extravagantly out of context with our economic system that it is effectively unusable, obsolete, and totally broken. There is a growing segment of Americans who are beset with "financial insufficiency for adequate societal integration." Minimum-wage scales are so low that low-wage earners must get help from one or more social safety net programs.

We really do live in a $20-per-hour-plus society. If this were a part of our economic infrastructure, we possibly could "eliminate" many of the federal and state welfare programs, close down volumes of the administrative welfare offices, and literally terminate dozens of low-income programs for every state in the nation. If the truth were to be told, probably the savings in administrative costs alone for the various welfare programs could cover much of the cost of boosting full-time, hardworking low-income earners to boot.

When you consider how a program such as the "earned income tax credit" plan would work, you would think it sounds efficient, effective, and economical, considering the position we find ourselves in. How so? Efficient in that the system of filing yearly income tax is already in place. Effective, considering how much falsification is used by welfare recipients and administrators alike. Economical in several ways, such as encouraging people to work, thereby reducing otherwise additional welfare claimants, reducing crime, greatly reduced cost by eliminating administration offices and associated costs.

It is written, "You will always have the poor among you." That is undoubtedly a fact. To think that we could close down every assistance office is unrealistic. To hope that we could greatly trim welfare cost by rewarding work sounds plausible and probably deserves debate.

Heroes They Are Not

The economic readjustment policy of world leadership in general has to remind us of the psychotic nurse who is obsessed with being a hero. It goes like this. The nurse gives the patient a nearly lethal injection and implements a plan to save their victim, and then take credit for performing what appears to be a heroic action.

Our politicians work overtime to drive labor rates to the bottom by signing trade deals that de-capitalize our economy, and then implement welfare programs to "save" the struggling American workers who are down and out from corporate export of wealth and jobs that they nodded their heads to.

As Dennis Kucinich, Democratic congressman from Ohio and 2008 presidential candidate, said to the *Boston Globe*, "One of the greatest hoaxes of this campaign—everyone's for universal health care. It's like a mantra. But when you get into the details, you find out that all the other candidates are talking about maintaining the existing for-profit system."

Viggo Mortensen, a Hollywood celebrity known for his work in *The Lord of the Rings*, was almost a sole celebrity supporter who appeared at the New Hampshire campaign for Mr. Kucinich. How much press coverage did Kucinich get?

I personally had to go to the Internet to view taped footage of him.

Do you think maybe his strong stance for a nonprofit health care system had anything to do with the press avoiding him, similarly to old fears associated with leprosy? He got so little publicity it looked like he was unable to raise enough corporate contributions to buy bus fare back to Ohio.

What he stood for certainly indicates why he got such little airtime and why he gained little financial support. As you have heard before, the media is by and large corporate America too.

As Kucinich said, everyone's for universal health care, meaning the public at large. Even when we the people have a candidate who echoes the views of a majority, major media is able to silence the voice of a champion of the cause simply by refusing to give equal airtime.

I hate to admit it, but we the people are easily influenced by the minority with the loudest voice. Corporate media are a sophisticated bunch that know how to do what they do best, and that is to tell those who don't possess self-conviction what they want us to believe, get us to nod our heads in agreement, and go around repeating what we heard as if it were the gospel.

A poll was taken in which it was reported that 70 percent of Americans were in favor of a single-payer not-for-profit health care system. With 70 percent in favor of health care reform (not health insurance reform), does it make you wonder why leadership is still advocating ever more insurance premium payment systems?

Let's face it. Our health care is broken, period. No matter what kind of a pay system we adopt, it's the cost of services, medications, and everything associated with health, hospitalization, and recovery that must be managed effectively to stamp out greed and fraud. Greed and fraud are so pervasive that it makes sense to concentrate on just these two things to combat out-of-control cost rather than attempts to initiate any new insurance or public option plan.

With all eyes on the 2007 United Auto Workers Union contract talks with the big three American car companies, who have said American car companies cannot compete with Asian and European companies that do not have the added costs of employee health care cost added to the price of every vehicle that comes off the production lines. Everyone was wondering what the unions would be pushing for in what could be said as the last-ditch effort to keep America in the manufacturing game.

The following is what was said by two of the most powerful and influential Union leaders in the UAW:

"There is a tremendous liability in projected health care costs for retirees," Ron Gettelfinger, President and Vice President General Holifield wrote. "America's health care crisis is out of control and that's why the UAW supports a national, single payer, comprehensive national health care plan for every man, woman and child. We cannot solve the health care crisis in any one set of negotiations with any one company."

There is no mistaking as to what the UAW wants Washington to do to get our health care crisis on what many believe is a better direction, and to put us on equal playing ground with other industrialized nations where health care coverage is a single-payer public-funded responsibility. As Kucinich stated, "everyone wants it."

"Isn't it time to look at the other models that exist that are workable for all the other industrialized nations in the world?" Kuninich makes a good point, but it appears imminently futile.

All the 2008 presidential candidates (except Dennis Kucinich, and he is out of the race) are talking as if the UAW was never heard of and does not exist. The UAW has become the tiger with no teeth.

During the George W. Bush Administration

In an article that first appeared in the *Boston Globe* around November 2006, written by Scot Lehigh, it states this: "The Chiefs of Ford, General Motors, and Chrysler went to Washington to meet with the president, the vice president, and various administration officials about the auto industry's woes."

And what did they suggest by way of a solution? Something John Kerry proposed during his presidential campaign (2004): a reinsurance arrangement to pay for chronic or catastrophic health care costs, thereby effectively taking those cases out of private health insurance plans.

This would amount to a partial universal health care plan. "One possibility they discussed conceptually was a pool to address the disproportionate costs associated with those who have chronic or serious illnesses," says Greg Martin, Washington spokesman for GM. (Determining chronic and serious should be interesting—my words.)

Can you see what is at work here? Kerry's plan keeps the insurance companies in the game, and in a way that they could cheer about, removing those catastrophic payouts from their bottom line. Now that really is putting them just where they want us, something for the insurance companies to really chuckle about when they get behind closed doors. Of course the Detroit auto companies would favor such a plan; it would remove much of the cost for employee coverage. That was easy.

But what does it do to lower costs to the American people and the costs for Carey's two-part, bureaucratic, paper-laden, administrative-heavy plan? Nothing. In fact, after the government (taxpayers) picks up catastrophic chronic and serious illness (socialism) payouts, thereby saving each premium payer 10 percent, it amounts to a windfall for the insurance folks and a horrendous amount paid out of tax-payer monies directly to doctors and hospitals for the big-ticket chronic and serious illnesses.

It isn't difficult to see through this one, folks. If Democrats are better at looking out for the little guy, this is a very poor example of it. They will come up with whatever it takes to keep the big insurance companies in the game, and even improve their position on the field.

The report says, "Now, Kerry's political stock isn't exactly soaring." But at a time when some on the left see a politically unattainable single-payer system as the only true solution to the nation's health care problems, and some on the right insist that impractical, unproven health savings accounts are the proper prescription, the senator's concept represents pragmatic middle ground.

When you take into account the billions that would come from taxpayers picking up the tab for chronic and seri-ous illnesses, 10 percent savings on existing premiums is a lot less than a "pragmatic, practical middle ground." It is a good thing that Teresa Heinz Kerry is in charge at Heinz rather than Mr. Kerry, or the Heinz Company would be at risk of existing.

No one is stepping on the toes of the insurance bosses. I think that the evidence overwhelmingly indicates that the insurance companies are in charge of allowing what gets put on the table. After a while, it always comes back to who really rules the world? I am prone to suggest that insurance companies wield heavy influence in their economic sector that amounts to what I term *corporate communism.*

Dennis Kucinich has got it right: "Some want to make it mandatory for people to have health insurance, but what they are not mandating is the money insurance companies can make. People can have health insurance, but be in worse shape after treatment with the deductibles, co-pays, and premiums. It should be a basic right in a democratic society, not a privilege based on your ability to pay."

If we continue to support a health care system that indeed provides a higher level of care to those who can afford to pay, it says a lot about what we as a society are.

The Rest of the Story

In all of America, we do not have one single economic problem or funding short fall that cannot be directly or indirectly connected to the failure of Washington leadership to set the tone throughout the world, that would have eased poverty around the globe at a much-faster pace than any of the results produced through their rhetorical propaganda for free trade that, historically, has been proven, in most cases, to be complete failures, especially between unequally yoked partners.

To say that war on the middle class in the economic sense does not do justice to the wholesale transfer of millions of jobs and billions of dollars and unfathomable wealth that has left American National Security in the balance. Over the past forty years, corporate America was given a free pass under the guise of free trade. There is little doubt in the mind of this writer that the imperfect partnership between we the people, corporate America, and the Washington establishment became obscured by greed, confusing those who took an oath to serve "we the people".

About the Author

If you really want to learn what war is about, it is best to hear it from a war veteran—not politicians, the grand kids, or the media.

War on the middle class was a different kind of war. No bombs were dropped or shots fired, but there were victims and there were survivors. American workers by the hundreds, and then by the thousands, and then by the millions adjusted to having no jobs or a new job and, in many cases, adjusting to resettlement, reestablishing a new place to call home, and making hard lifestyle changes based on their attempts to maintain a compromised standard of living or adjusting to the de-capitalization of America as a whole.

War on the middle class was never viewed as a holocaust, and those so affected were never referred to as refugees. However, after all things considered, the author asks those who will read *Imperfect Partners,* what would you call this life-altering experience?

The author has thirty-four years of experience working in heavy industry, being on the ground as shrinking "Made in the USA" began with outsourcing, followed by relocating bits and pieces of the businesses that were more profitable done offshore, and finally exporting entire manufacturing capability to foreign places.

As the author researched the outsourcing process that brought America to her manufacturing knees, it became imperative that the story of the victims of this silent war on the middle class deserves to be told in a manner that reflects the great sacrifices endured by millions of America's hardworking people.

The author dug deeply to discover behind-the-scenes activities initiated by corporate America partnering with not only our own political system but also inclusive of world systems created exclusively for the effort in fostering the new global economy and establishing a new world order.

When it is all said and done, has the alliance between corporate America and the political system carried out a campaign that could be described as having *political and economic terrorism* effects?